MAI

WORI

Bernard Onyiwe

Dream Beyond Limits

© 2022 **Europe Books**| London
www.europebooks.co.uk | info@europebooks.co.uk

ISBN 9791220119436
First edition: April 2022
Distribution for the United Kingdom: **Vine House
Distribution ltd**

Printed for Italy by Rotomail Italia
Finito di stampare presso Rotomail Italia S.p.A. - Vignate (MI)

Dream Beyond Limits

This book is dedicated to the glory of the Almighty God for the inspiration and ability to write it.

I also want to dedicate this book to the loving memory of my late father Benson Onyiwe. His early demise did leave a big vacuum in my life, but I thank God for filling that vacuum.

My special thank goes to my wonderful wife Chinwe Onyiwe and our beautiful children for all their support in my life and ministry.

I have been a student under the teachings of great men of God and I want to thank all my fathers in the Lord starting from the General Overseer of the Redeemed Christian church of God Pst. E.A Adeboye and his wife Pst. Mrs Folu Adeboye. My regional pastor, Pst. Idowu Iluyomade, our intercontinental Youth pastor, Pst. Belemina Obunge, my provincial pastor, Pst. Bisi Akande and his assistant Pst. Felix Oni and all pastors working with them, my father, friend, and coach Pst. Adewale Adesola and others too numerous to mention.

Finally, I want to specially thank my daughter Vanilla Onyiwe for her contribution in her own little way in putting this book together. She was indeed reliable and dependable.

God bless you all.

The seat of knowledge is the Head, the seat of Wisdom is the Heart. Until you move what you have in your head to your heart knowledge is useless. When you are armed with wisdom you rule every aspect of life.

INDEX

FORWARD

This book "Dream Beyond Limits" is a product of my 12 years as a pastor working with the Youths and Young Adults.

In the course of these 12 years, I have worked with these young ones, males and females. We organised programs like Youth Conventions, Mission outreach, Seminars etc., together and having to speak to them I discovered that a lot of them have potentials hidden inside of them and a lot did not know what to do.

This book is expected to spur them and anyone who reads it to think outside the Box considering the fact that they are more than the degree or qualifications they all carry about.

The purpose of Education is to make individuals see the creative abilities that lie within them. Dream Beyond Limits is expected to make you see that in yourself. This book is to educate, enlighten and inform you that your minds are like the Parachute which only works when it is open.

The Bible in the book of Romans 12:2, says "And be not conformed to this world: but be ye transformed by the renewing of your mind, that ye may prove what is that good, and acceptable, and perfect, will of God.

So, this book starts with Chapter one by addressing the mind because the truth is all battles of life starts from the mind. Yes, the world would want us to conform becoming what it wants us to be. But God wants us to be transformed by the renewing of our minds through the word of God. Becoming exactly what He wants us to be. We know there are obstacles, challenges on the way but these challenges are not peculiar to you, others have encountered same and overcame.

Chapter 2 encourages us to dream, and to dream big. We serve a Big God who is ready to help us all the way. When your dream is small you don't really need God. You need God when you have a very big dream and you know you cannot actualize that dream on your own. In the book of Isiah chapter 41:13, God was speaking, 'For I am the LORD your God   who takes hold of your right hand
and says to you, Do not fear; I will help you.

God is not a man, so if He says He is going to help you, it means He will be helping you, so don't short change yourself, dream big.

Chapter 3 encourages you to plan your journey. This time your life's journey. You are encouraged to break your dream into goals and have a plan on how to actualize each goal you have set for yourself.

In Chapter 4 we talk about you minding your association, those who you call your friends. You don't have business hanging out with people who are not going your way. Some persons will just waste your time. Time is key here, The same time you spend on things that are not adding value to you is the same time needed to actualize your goals, 'Time is Money'.

In chapter 5 we address the most important ingredient in your success-YOU. Some things will not happen quickly, suddenly, as soon as, immediately. They will have to go through a process. One of those things has to be your growth. It takes a life time to be a successful person. We are work in progress. Yes, Rome was not built a day, but what are you ready to give for your growth? Your growth in life must be intentional. Your improvement in life must be intentional. No one improves by accident.

Chapter 6 talks about you saying it. Talking about your dream, there is power in your word. God is not only interested in hearing what we say, He is equally interested in ensuring that we get what we say. So, you are advised not to speak evil about yourself, but to build your world with your word because "your word is your world".

In chapter 7 we are encouraged to get down and work the dream out. It is not enough to have a big dream, but working it out, little by little no matter how small, just start. People will laugh at you, talk down on you, but don't let people's opinion about you kill your dream, just push on. A lot of dreams have been killed by laughter, yours don't have to die.

The book is concluded in chapter 8 which talks on "expect it". It encourages us to be expectant. Just like a pregnant woman is said to be expectant of a baby, we are encouraged to expect results. Having done all we can do, we look up to God to bring the increase. He sees our hurts, He sees the tears and He is ever ready to help us. All we need to do is to believe and call on Him.

Some things will not happen on their own, Unless God helps you. Genesis 27:20- Isaac asked his son, "How did you find it so quickly, my son?" "The LORD your God gave me success," he replied.

Everyone has a destiny to fulfil in Christ. But not everyone fulfils their destiny. Destiny is first and foremost the original intention of God for your life. It includes the purpose, place and program for your life. One way to fulfil Purpose in life is by PRAYER- Psalms 37:5 - Commit your way to the LORD; trust in him and he will bring it to pass. It is my prayer for you that as you trust the Lord, the wind that is meant to stop you will push you into your destiny in Jesus Mighty name.

CHAPTER ONE

RESET YOUR MIND

The human mind is the most powerful tool available to mankind. Nothing happens with a man whose mind is asleep, he would not move, he wouldn't eat, he wouldn't be able to do anything for himself or others. He is just there!

A man whose mind is dead, is indeed, a dead man.

Imagine all the cures for various ailments, great inventions and discoveries mankind has been able to accomplish.

The automobile, electricity, train, airplane, sending a man to the moon and space, the massive breakthroughs (in Science, Technology and Finance) etc. All these were achieved by the human mind because someone first thought about it.

Until you start thinking, nobody will respect you. The day you have a thought revolution every other thing will change. It is only a good thinking that will produce a good life. What is the worth of your thought life? Your mental picture determines your life picture. The state of your thoughts is the state of your life. You cannot live outside of your thoughts. You cannot be bigger than how you think.

Proverb 23:7a (NKJV)-For as he thinks in his heart, so *is* he.

You think people do not associate with you or dislike you because of your race, your colour, your family background, your academic background, your body physique: Too fat, too slim, too short or too tall, because of a disability or another, whatever?

People can say whatever they want to say concerning you. They have a right to their own opinion concerning you. They can call you whatever they want to call you. It doesn't matter. What matters is what you call yourself. You are what you answer to.

Every limitation that you see, is that which you have put there yourself. It all starts in your mind! Whatever you see as a challenge today, someone else experienced or suffered same and a lot overcame it.

For you, growing up as a child you once had some crazy dreams when you told the adults about it, they asked you to be real. And in being real you had to jettison or killed those dreams. You did that because they called you names, they told you that you were out of your mind. They told you, the dream was not feasible because no one in your family had been able to achieve that feat. They told you it was not possible because they felt they knew you far better than you know yourself.

Words are like seeds, you dwell on them too long and they will develop a root and grow and before you know it, they will become your reality. The battle of life is in your mind. Everyone is entitled to what they think of you.

Romans 12:2 (NIV) "Do not conform to the pattern of this world but be transformed by the renewing of your mind. Then you will be able to test and approve what

God's will is--his good, pleasing and perfect will." Then you will learn to know God's will for you, which is good and pleasing and perfect."

Conforming simply put is to act in accordance with expectations, to behave in the manner of others, especially because of social pressure. To be in accordance with a set of specifications or regulations.

To transform, on the other hand, means to change greatly the appearance or form of a thing. It means a deliberate intention to change the status quo.

What do you feed your mind with? They might have told you different stories of what you can achieve and become. They could have told you these things in good fate. It could have been from your parents, friends, neighbors, coach or even a Spiritual leader. What people say about you does not really matter, what matters is what you say concerning yourself and what God says about you.

It is time you start purging your mind of some things. Read God's word concerning you. Mind what you see or look, what you listen to and what you say about yourself. It is wrong you saying something bad about someone, it is equally wrong you saying bad things about yourself. You have so much against you, please don't add to it.

2Timothy 1:7 (NKJV)- "For God has not given us a spirit of fear, but of power and of love and of a sound mind".

The story is told of a research conducted in the US by some Scientist on 8 monkeys. At the beginning they had four of these monkeys in a cage and at the top of the cage they put some bananas knowing how monkeys love bananas the monkeys wanted some. So, one the monkeys made an attempt going for the bananas, on getting to the top as it attempted to get some of the bananas the Scientist poured very cold water on the monkey. It ran back down.

A second monkey then attempted, it went up the cage and on getting to the top as it also tried to pick a banana the Scientist also poured it some cold water. It ran back down the cage.

The Scientist observed that no other monkey tried reaching for the bananas. After some time, the Scientist removed the 2 monkeys that had the experience of the cold water and replaced them with 2 other monkeys. They observed for a while and noticed that no monkey attempted to reach for the bananas. So, they removed the other 2 monkeys that were in the cage when the monkeys had the cold-water experience and replaced them with other 2 monkeys and also observed for some time. They observed that even though the 4 monkeys now in the cage were not there when they poured the cold water on those two monkeys, yet none went for the bananas.

What happened? The Scientist concluded that the information was passed from the initial 4 monkeys to these new 4 monkeys.

A lot of the things we believe are things we have no knowledge about. We just believe them because we were told that's how things are.

Some of these things are not real, some of them are mere superstitious but because they were told by a respectable person, parent, teacher, coach or a Spiritual leader we just swallow them hook, line and sinker.

Things are not what they seem they are. It is time you begin to clear your mind of those strongholds that have held you down for long.

2Corinthians 10:4 (NKJV) – "For the weapons of our warfare *are* not carnal but mighty in God for pulling down strongholds, what has limited you all this while was your mind. You believe you can make it, you are right, you can. You believe you cannot make it, you are also right, you can't. Remember "as he thinks in his heart so is he."

God will normally call you away from the familiar because the familiar will normally talk you out of your dream e.g., Abraham, Jacob and Joseph. It is time you begin to check those you listen to. Stay away from people who will tell you to commit abortion. They would want you to abort your dreams by their negative words. Move with people who are also pregnant with dreams.

You have a seed of greatness inside of you, there is something unique about you. God knows what you are capable of. Men will always want to put off your fire, kill that seed of greatness. But if you can shake that off like David in the Bible, you will rise up and go on to become what God wants you to be.

When God was tired of having Saul as king over Israel, he asked the prophet Samuel to go to the house of Jesse to anoint him a new king. On the day Samuel arrived all Jesse's sons were present except David. After Jesse had made the 7 of them go before Samuel and God turning them down or rejecting them, Samuel asked 'are these all your sons?' Jesse answered there remains one, but he is in the field attending to the sheep.

The question is why did Jesse leave David out on this great day? A day when a new king over the whole of Israel was to be anointed. The answer is simply because he did not believe in him. He was a child, not experienced. Does not have the desired skill set, he was just a shepherd boy. 1Samuel 16:11 (NKJV) -And Samuel said to Jesse, "Are all the young men here?" Then he said, "There remains yet the youngest, and there he is, keeping the sheep."

And Samuel said to Jesse, "Send and bring him. For we will not sit down till he comes here."

Yes, his father did not believe in him, his brethren doubted what he could do but he never doubted himself or what God was capable of doing through him. No wonder he said in the book of Psalms 139:14 (NKJV) - I will praise you, for I am fearfully *and* wonderfully made; marvellous are your works, and *that* my soul knows very well.

Yes, he knew he was fearfully and wonderfully made, he knew he had greatness in him, he knew he was a giant killer and was going to be a great king.

Imagine yourself without hands and legs, and all you have is your mind. Well stop imagining. This is the life of a man Nick Vujicic (pronounced 'vooycheech'). His name may not ring a bell for many around the world, but if we refer to him as a motivational speaker and a CEO of two companies who is without arms and legs, then many of you would instantly place him through his amazing videos and extremely motivational videos on the social media.

Nick, who was born with tetra-amelia syndrome, a rare disorder characterised by the absence of all four limbs, has over 1.6 million followers on Instagram and his videos on YouTube have inspired millions with his message to love life and live without limits.

At birth, his mother refused to see or hold him. At school he was tormented so much that at the age of 10 he attempted suicide by drowning himself in a bathtub. But he realised that he could not torture his family more by ending his life in that manner.

The turning point for the young boy battling years of loneliness and low self-esteem came when at 13 he hurt his foot which he was using for writing and swimming. This made him realise that he needed to be thankful for his abilities rather than focusing on his disabilities. Motivated by a janitor he started sharing his story with people and soon the numbers grew, and he has delivered nearly 2,000 talks across the globe and has also written four books. His undying faith removed all anxiety about his uncertain life and gave new hope for happiness.
Nick is the founder of two companies — Life without limbs (in which he is presently the CEO) and Attitude is the altitude. Nick has been married since 2012 and has a beautiful supporting wife and four kids.
Nick's life story is the best example of what human grit and determination can achieve. He is a living proof of how one can face any adversity and achieve the unachievable. One should not focus on what one is lack-

ing but should rather have gratitude for what one has and put it to the best use and never shirk from hard work and never lose confidence in oneself.

William James said, "The greatest discovery of my generation is that men can change their circumstances by changing their attitude of mind."

Nick is a highly inspiring person not because of the companies he owns or the books he wrote, but because of "how" he did all that and the difference that he has made to millions of people's lives.

The turning point was right in his mind. He believed he could use his circumstances to encourage someone, to inspire someone. Just like Nick, if you also believe you can turn what appears as a stumbling block to a steppingstone.

Jesus was speaking in Matthew 9:29b, "According to your faith be it unto you."

From this Scripture and Proverb 23:7a we quoted earlier, it is obvious that as a man we always act on the outside based on our innermost beliefs and convictions about ourselves. No wander the most important of all mental laws is the law of beliefs. This law according to Brian Tracy, says that whatever you believe with conviction becomes your reality. So, in essence, you do not believe what you see; you see what you believe. We actually view our world through a lens of beliefs, Attitudes, prejudices and preconceived notions.

So, you are not what you think you are, but what you think, you are!

If your mind was not important the Bible will not ask you to have the same mind as Christ in the book of Philippian 2:5 (NKJV) – "Let this mind be in you which was also in Christ Jesus". This simply tells us to have a mind-set like Christ, to think and act like Christ does.

It means bringing every faculty of our mind to bear on how we actually can have the mind of Christ.

It means that for every situation you find yourself, ask, what will Jesus do if he were in my shoes? Would he be shouting and wailing? Would he be calling a friend to complain? Would he be feeling dejected and inferior? Or would he be speaking to the situation?

Ephesians 1: 18 (NKJV) – "The eyes of your understanding being enlightened; that you may know what the hope of His calling is, what are the riches of the glory of His inheritance in the saints

You want to live beyond every limitation? Your inner eyes must be able to see clearly. If you can't see it, you can't have it. You may not see it with your physical eyes, but do you see it with your inner eyes?"

Jeremiah 5:21 (NKJV)- "Hear this now, O foolish people,
Without understanding, who have eyes and see not, and who have ears and hear not:

God expects us to be creative, Creativity gives our eyes ability to see beyond the common phenomenon. Eyes that look are common, eyes that see are rare!"

Marcus Aurelius (wisest emperor of Rome) said, "A man's life is what his thought made of Him." Your MENTALITY is your REALITY.

You can think yourself into or out of any situation. You can make yourself sick with your thought and you can also make yourself well with your thought.

Brian Tracy said, "It is not what happens to you that matter, but how you think about what happens to you that determines how you feel and react."

Discovering consist of seeing what everybody has seen but thinking what nobody has thought. Begin to see beyond your present to behold opportunity for innovation and creativity in every task that confronts you on the way of Success.

Helen Keller was once asked 'What is worse than being born blind? 'Her answer was remarkable, she said, 'having Eyes that cannot see '.

The story is told of a young man working with a cold room company in the US as a technician. One day his Boss called him to check one of the Vans whose cooling system was faulty at about 4pm.

He took his tools a pen and a jotter and went to the van. The van could only be opened from the outside and not from the inside. On entering the trunk of the van, he forgot to hook the door. As he started troubleshooting the cooling system of the Van to troubleshoot why it was not working, the door came down and locked. He was trapped inside the trunk of the van. He called for help, but no one heard him. Not long he heard the closing bell rang and soon people rushing to leave for the day.

Not long he heard the last footstep leave the company for that day, immediately it dawned on him he was inside the trunk of a mobile cold room. He thought within himself, the temperature of a cold room can reach -10 degrees, am going to freeze to death he said to himself.

After a while, he wrote on his jotter, it is quite cold in here, I think am going to freeze to death.

By the next day, his colleagues were looking for him. His boss reminded them his last assignment the previous day was to check the faulty cooling unit of a van. They went for the van and lo, he was there in his coverall with his written note by his side, dead.

The autopsy report clearly stated that he died of extreme cold. They checked the cooling unit of the van, it was still faulty not working. So, the question is "what killed him?"

His mind killed him. He thought of himself dying of extreme cold and his mind was able to generate the extreme cold capable of killing him.

Our mind is basically divided into 2 compartments, the conscious and the subconscious mind.

The conscious mind is what you and I have control over. We control our conscious mind by what we feed it. What we see, what we hear and most importantly what we say. The conscious mind is master over the subconscious mind which is a slave. The subconscious mind carries out activities based on the information received from the conscious mind. So, if what you feed the conscious mind are the negatives, impossible. That is what you will get as that's what the subconscious will carry out.

Also, if you are an optimistic person seeing the right side of things, as you say this to yourself you pass the same information to the conscious mind which eventually relays it to the subconscious and before you know it, things start turning around for you.

Psalms 45:1, talks about our tongue being the pen of a ready writer, the pen writes on a book, where does your tongue write? Yes, on the tables of your heart, hence the need to guide your heart with all diligence. So be mindful what you write on it.

Back home in Nigeria in one of our parishes, we had a Sister who suffered Leukemia (cancer of the blood). The doctors asked the husband to take her home and gave her a death date (the date she was supposed to die). She was emaciated. When she returned home, we went to pay our visit and pray with her. She was always saying, 'this is just a phase after this season I will be fine.' I told those who went with me that the sister was not going to die. They asked me how I knew that. My answer was just listening to her (seasons do change). It is 16 years after and she is still alive.

You want to know what your life will look like 5 years from now. Just listen to yourself.

What is that which is still holding you down? Clear your mind, reset it with the word of God. Proverbs 4:23 (NKJV)- "Keep your heart with all diligence,
For out of it *spring* the issues of life. You cannot leave outside your thought."

Romans 9:13 (NKJV)- As the Scriptures say, "I loved Jacob, but I hated Esau."

What could Esau have done that even before he was born God hated him?

You can only answer this if you know God to be the Omniscient, the all-knowing God. Only one who knows the ending from the beginning.

In Genesis 25 the Bible recorded that Esau despised his birth right, he sold it for a plate of food.

Till today, there are two kinds of people and 2 kinds of nations in the world, the Esau people and the Jacob people. The Esau nations and the Jacob nations.

The Esau's depends on Physical strength, while the Jacobs rely on mind strength.

The Bible recorded that Esau was rugged while Jacob was refined.

Proverbs 12:27(KJV) -The slothful man roasteth not that which he took in hunting: but the substance of a diligent man is precious.

The Jacobs provide food for the Esau's of this world. The Esau's Pay to the Jacobs of this world.

The Esau's ask God for a forest and turn it to a desert- They Kill whatever they catch while the Jacobs ask God for a seed and turn it into a forest. They cultivate what they have.

Check out most African Nations- Nigeria is blessed with oil, Ghana with Cocoa and Gold, Botswana with Diamonds, Democratic Republic of Congo with Diamonds and Copper, South Africa – Diamonds, Gold, Aluminum, Copper, Platinum, and Coal. Tanzania with Gold, Namibia with Uranium. Mozambique with Aluminum, Zambia with Copper, Guinea with Bauxite.

Esau Nations provide the raw materials but too lazy to refine it.

Laziness is not the inability to work but the inability to complete work. Nobody eats raw meat.

Best chocolate is from Switzerland, Switzerland does not grow Cocoa, best wristwatch from Switzerland, no African nation produces wristwatch.

Singapore is just a city state, but her GDP is more than that of Africa as a continent.

Life is not about what you have caught, but what you can roast.

Nigeria has oil yet each year Nigerians queue for fuel, she can only boast of four nonfunctional refineries.

God said I love Jacob- He was talking about the mind set and attitude of Jacob.

The wealth of Esau was in the field, but the wealth of Jacob was in His head.

Esau would use all his strength to chase one game and eventually when he catches it, HE KILLS it.

The bane of most African countries is the natural resources they are endowed with. This has resulted to so much corruption and political killings. When you see a politician who steals all that belongs to his country, his state or local government and buries it in a pit he calls a Dollar farm, starving his people that is an Esau mind set. God says I hate Esau.

Jacob grows the little he has until it becomes mighty in his hand, but Esau work hard to only kill that which he caught.

Hard work without sense is punishment to the body, it is called labor. In the school of efficiency there is no friction. Sweating is a sign that something is not right. Start using more of your head and less of strength. It is not great events that makes a man it is great decisions.

Are you a Jacob or an Esau? Is your country run by Esau's or a Jacob? Esau died as Esau Jacob died as Israel. When you start using your head God makes a new man out of you.

It is my prayer for you that as you have a mind reset today, you will start your journey to becoming what God has created you to be.

CHAPTER TWO

DREAM BIG

A man dies when he stops dreaming!

Ecclesiastes 5:3 (NIV)- "A dream comes when there are many cares, and many words mark the speech of a fool."

To dream is to be alive, to dream is to be wise.

What is a dream? What is a Vision? Do you have a vision or a dream for your life?

How much does it cost to dream? Why is it that some persons do not dream?

All these we will try and answer in this chapter.

Job 33:15 -16 (NIV)-

¹⁵ In a dream, in a vision of the night,
when deep sleep falls on people
as they slumber in their beds,
¹⁶ he may speak in their ears
and terrify them with warnings,

You had a nightmare if your dream is not different compared to your present reality. When you dream you should see yourself doing great things you are not doing now. A dream should tell you there is something great ahead of you otherwise you just had a nightmare.

Psalms 126:1 (AMP) – "When the LORD brought back the captives to Zion (Jerusalem), we were like those who dream [it seemed so unreal]."

What this scripture means, is that whenever you dream you should be doing better than your present reality.

Dreams and Visions are similar in so many ways. They talk about your ability to see, an idea or picture in your imagination, the ability to think about or plan the future with great imagination and intelligence. They are mental pictures of your future. They are like an address to your destination, even though you have not been there.

The difference between the two are:

1. A dream is much bigger than a Vision, it out-lives the dreamer. A vision is the indebt capacity of measurable impact of a dream.
   Abraham had a dream in Genesis 15:12-18. God interpreted his dream informing him his descendants would be oppressed in a foreign land after four hundred years He would bring them out and punish the nation that oppressed them. Long after Abraham had died and buried, the dream came to pass.
   Joseph had 2 dreams in Genesis 37:5-11. His dreams outlived him. After many years when he was about to die, he told his brethren not to bury him in Egypt but instructed them to take his bones with them when they are leaving Egypt.
2. According to Joel 2:38(NIV)- "And afterward, I will pour out my Spirit on all people.

> Your sons and daughters will prophesy,
> your old men will dream dreams,
> your young men will see visions."

According to the Scripture above, dreams are for the old men and Visions are for the young men.

But for the purpose of this book, we will be treating visions and dreams as being the same.

Sometimes a dream is only a picture, an image that we don't fully understand and requires faith to believe in. God may give you a dream in pieces i.e., as visions—asking you to believe. As you take small steps in faith, he will fill in the gaps along the way.

This is what happened in Joseph's life in Genesis 37. God gave Joseph an unusual dream that he did not fully understand, but Joseph immediately believed. And because of it, Joseph's brothers hated him, and his father scolded him. No one believed Joseph, and for years and years his dream made his life really difficult. Betrayed and left for dead by his brothers, sold into slavery in a foreign land, alone and afraid, all Joseph had to hold on to be his dream and his faith in God. But Joseph would not let go of it, and little by little he began to see hints and clues that his dream was coming true.

WHAT IS YOUR DREAM?

I am not talking about a wish — a wish is usually only a passing thought that most people never act on. But a dream is something that captures your heart and spirit. It ignites your imagination and fills you with an unquenchable hope. It becomes something you cannot easily set aside.

Dreams consume your thinking and fuel your excitement and passion. It can happen in a single moment, or it can captivate your thoughts for years. Sometimes when the dream is really big, you embrace it, and somehow it feels like the dream embraces you.

Our dreams are often about experiencing a better life, about achieving greater things ... they are pictures we have of the future that reveal a part of our lives that will be greater than the past.

It cost nothing to dream. But we still have a lot who do not dream.

Well, it takes courage to dream. Any time you dare to dream, there are risks involved. What if it never happens? What if it costs too much to actualize? What if people laugh at you?

It's hard to hold on to your dreams. It's hard to believe when the world and those around you give you no reason to press in and press on.

As a child what was your dream? When you told your guardians or your friends, did they ask you to be real? Well, I have good news for you, for the fact that you abandoned that dream does not mean that God gave up on the dream. You can pick it up again today.

I have been blessed to realize many dreams in my life, and I'm convinced that a dream only happens when two things take place:

Firstly, you need Faith and secondly you need patience.

Hebrews 6:12(NIV) - We do not want you to become lazy, but to imitate those who through faith and patience inherit what has been promised.

I lost my Father when I was just four years old. Growing up was tough. Family members after my Primary school wanted me to learn tailoring [my father's trade]. Somehow, I wanted to go to school, to a university something no one in my family before me had done.

I was unsure how it would happen. But I just kept believing God's Word. He encouraged me that with Him "nothing was impossible." As months went by, there were many times when the obstacles and problems outnumbered the possibilities for me to receive the promise, He had given me.

But during these times, I went to God's Word and learned something from the life of David. In I Samuel 30:6, it says that David encouraged himself in the Lord.

So, I made the decision that when circumstances or people said things that discouraged the dreams in my heart, I would go back to the Lord and stand on His promises. Beyond that, I would do everything I could to continually express hope, both verbally and in my actions, in what I believed God had in store for me.

I chose NOT to let go of the dream or give up, but to press on and praise God.

I wish that everyone could have an encouraging voice like that in their life, but sometimes it's not always the case. In fact, sometimes those closest to you can actually be the biggest "unbelievers" of your dreams.

In Genesis 37:5-20, this was exactly what happened to Joseph. His brethren did not believe the dreams, in fact they hated him for it.

What is the vision or dream from God that's captured your heart, that's lingered, that won't go away? Are you still holding on to it or have you let it go? If you have, the time has come to pick it back up again and reclaim your dream. That is what Joseph did.

The challenges you face will require you to make a similar choice — will you leave your pain in the past to follow your dreams, or will you let these hurts steal your hope of a better life?

As I said, seeing your dream come to pass may not be easy, but once it does, it is totally worth everything you have invested into it.

Dreaming and believing for better things in your life and the lives of those around you is contagious. When you get around someone with the courage to dream, it has an amazing impact on you.

Mary went to Elizabeth and the baby in Elizabeth's womb leaped. Who are those you go to? Those that make your baby to sleep or those who make your baby leap?

As believers, we do not put our trust in circumstances or people. Our trust remains in the Lord. God is able to do exceedingly abundantly more than we can ask or think. This is what we are believing for, and I am confident that it will happen as we join hands and hearts to offer real hope to people ... hope that can only be found in a personal relationship with Jesus Christ.

Don't let anything hold you back. Don't let anyone keep you from dreaming. The dreams God has given you are treasures worth living for. They are worth the price, I promise.

I read the story of a young British Afghan NHS doctor Waheed Arian who was born in Afghanistan in 1983, the last of a family of ten. During the Soviet-Afghan conflict he and his family were constantly moving as a result of the conflict. At a time, he moved with the family to Pakistan where they all stayed in a single room there, he suffered Tuberculosis (TB), malaria and malnutrition. It was during this period that he dreamt of becoming a medical doctor to also save lives. After the war, at age 15, his father sent him to the United Kingdom to seek asylum.

He arrived into the UK with just $100 in his pocket. He worked in shops to support himself and send money back to his family. Arian began studying at three separate colleges in the evening. With five A Levels, Arian was accepted by the University of Cambridge to study medicine. He found himself very socially isolated in his two years, his background setting him apart from his fellow students. His main friend was a kitchen porter at the university, whom he felt he had more in common with. Arian subsequently received more support from university and formed links through setting up Afghan and martial arts societies.

He graduated from Cambridge in 2006 with a science degree and went on to finish his clinical studies at imperial college London then winning a scholarship to take an elective in surgery at Harvard Medical School in the US in 2008.

In 2009 he founded the Arian Teleheal which is an online medical service connecting Volunteer doctors in the UK, US and Canada to doctors in Syria, Afghanistan and many 3rd world countries. The service began supporting the Independent Doctors' Association in Syria, supporting 1.3 million people, both locals and the internally displaced Syrian refugees.

An audit by the Afghanistan Ministry of Public Health found that, between 2016 and 2019, the advice given by Arian Teleheal volunteer medics had helped local doctors save 686 lives out of 779 life-threatening situations, a success rate of 88%.

Waheed Arian had a dream and with desire, discipline, and self-determination he birthed it to life. Today he is a recipient of several awards in the United Kingdom and abroad.

Nelson Mandela said, 'It always seems **impossible** until it's done.'

Walt Disney also said, 'the only way to discover the limits of the possible is to go beyond them into the **impossible**.'

According to St. Francis of Assisi, 'Start by **doing** what's necessary; then do what's possible; and suddenly you are **doing the impossible**. ...

A dream is only a dream until you give life to it.

DO NOT SETTLE FOR LESS.

The scripture talks about the children of Israel in the wilderness. They were fed by God. He gave them manner, sent them quails, and gave them water.

When it was time to go and take the Promise Land, they felt it was not worth it. After all we are okay here, they said.

You shouldn't be pitching tents, when you should be building houses, don't take God's temporal provision as a permanent destination.

A lot have settled for God's temporal provision instead of seeking for his greater gift. The scripture said "eyes has not seen, ear has not heard neither has it come to the heart of men what God has in store for them that love him" (1Corintians 2:9).

On the 10th of December 1914, the factory of Thomas Edison the famous inventor was engulfed in flames.

Later, at the scene of the blaze, Edison was quoted in The New York Times as saying, "Although I am over 67 years old, I'll start all over again tomorrow." He told the reporter that he was exhausted from remaining at the scene until the chaos was under control, but he stuck to his word and immediately began rebuilding the next morning.

According to Ryan Holiday, 'To do great things, we need to be able to endure tragedy and setbacks,"

The Lord wants you to remain on top in spite of the many events occurring in your life. The good breaks and the bad ones, the ups and the downs.
Many a times it appears we are making 1 step forward and 2 steps backwards.
Just like Joseph if you can hold on you will surely come through.

For a man with a Dream, the bigger the why, the easier the How.

The challenges you face will require you to make a similar choice — will you leave your pain in the past to follow your dreams, or will you let these hurts steal your hope of a better life?

As I said, seeing your dream come to pass may not be easy, but once it does, it is totally worth everything you have invested into it.

You must learn to stand like a wall when water is poured on you to attain your dream in life.

Your life will follow your dreams. If your dream is small, you will have a small life. If you have a limited dream, you will have a limited life. If you can achieve your dream without stretching your faith, then your dream is small, and you don't need God. Have a big vision, dream big. If you can see the invisible, then God can do the impossible.

Proverbs 22:2(NIV) – "Rich and poor have this in common:
 The LORD is the Maker of them all."

Proverbs 29:13(NIV) – "The poor and the oppressor have this in common:
The LORD gives sight to the eyes of both."

Who is the oppressor of the poor? Of course, the Rich. So, if God created both the rich and the poor, and gives eyes to both the rich and the poor, why is the poor man poor and the rich man rich?

The answer is in what they see. The rich man sees wealth of opportunities around him while the poor man sees nothing but poverty and misery.

Your life is not going to change unless you begin to change your pictures.
Your life will always follow the pictures you see.

Once again I tell you," If you can see the invisible God can do the impossible."
Life will always want to push you down but if you have a vision for your life, you will always fight your way back up.
Proverbs 24:16a (NIV)- "For though the righteous fall seven times, they rise again"

Ordinary men are never great. For you to be great you need to be extra-ordinary. You must begin to see what ordinary men can't see.

Proverbs 25:2 (NIV)- "It is the glory of God to conceal a matter;
   to search out a matter is the glory of kings.

WHAT SHOULD I DO WITH MY DREAM?

First Visualize it. Put your dreams in pictures. See yourself achieving that dream business, dream car, dream house, dream family, dream trip etc.

In Genesis chapter 15:5, God was speaking to Abraham, and he asked him to look at the sky and count the stars. Abraham could not and He told him "So shall thy seed be." On another occasion, he took him to the seashore and asked him to count the sand on the seashore. Why did God give Abraham pictures? It is because what you see matters. Proverbs 29:18a (KJV) - Where there is no vision, the people perish:

You cannot feature in a picture you have not pictured.

A lot have never seen themselves succeeding in life and so have always failed. They see setbacks, failures, addictions, immorality, abuses etc.

Change this picture. See yourself as God sees you. Have a picture of you been blessed, see yourself getting married, see yourself having your own children, see yourself buying that new car, see yourself owning your own house, see yourself passing that exam, see yourself getting that promotion, see yourself starting that business.

Seven times in the Bible God asked man, "what do you see?" Seven is a perfect number. So, we can say that God asked man a perfect question. Why would he do that? Because he knows what you see, determines what you get.

It is important, what you see because what you see determines what you can achieve in life. If you can see it, you can achieve it.

Secondly, write it down. Writing translates your imagination which is in the Spiritual to the physical.

Habakkuk 2:2 (NIV)-

Then the LORD replied:

"Write down the revelation
and make it plain on tablets
so that a herald may run with it."

Write your dreams down. There is this connection between your head and your hand. Writing your dreams down helps to bring the pictures from the invisible realm to the physical realm. It establishes what is referred to as a psycho-neuro activity.

When you commit something to writing, commitment to achievement naturally follows. And whenever you read and affirm positively out loud, your hope for accomplishment reinforced.

Even God wrote His vision for us in the form of the Bible. He does not solely depend on the Holy Spirit to guide us. He put His direction in writing.

We are also instructed to write down our vision in tablets. The importance of the Vision is to be able to RUN with it.

Thirdly, believe in your dream. Have faith in it. In order to give life to your dream you need to believe in it. No one would believe your dream if you don't. Even when others don't believe in it, you must believe that your dream will come through.

It's hard to hold on to your dreams. It's hard to believe when the world and those around you give you no reason to press in and press on.

That was exactly what Joseph did. Even when no one believed in his dream, he just held on.
Lastly, you need to be patient with your dream. Habakkuk 2:3 (NIV)-

"For the revelation awaits an appointed time;
 it speaks of the end
and will not prove false.
Though it linger, wait for it;
it[b] will certainly come
and will not delay."

WHAT WILL YOUR DREAM DO TO YOU?

1. It will contradict your present reality. It will always be different to what you see now. Any dream that looks like your present is a nightmare.
2. It will confront your sense of comfort, your sense of ease. It turns a spender into an investor. It will challenge your laziness. It will cause you to avoid time wasters. It does not procrastinate.
3. It conceives new opportunities. It will show you a way out of your complexities. A true dreamer cannot be stopped.
4. It will connect you to resources. Things will begin to work out for you. People will begin to connect to it.
5. It will help you conserve your energy. You will no longer hangout with people that drain your energy. In Mark chapter 5, a woman just touched Jesus and he said virtue had left him. Some people are like that, when they come around you, they just drain you. When your dream gets hold of you, you do not hang around such persons.

No one leaves you the same. Some will add to you while some will subtract from you. Associate with people that have dreams just like you.

It is a waste for a man to live another day without a Dream to accomplish.

Your existence should go beyond waking up, eating and sleeping. Your Existence should be impactful.

Your life should be ruled by a great passion to accomplish a Dream. Dream Big!

It is my prayer that as you begin to dream big. Expanding your Vision, God will release every resources you need unto you, and you will go on to become what God has created you to be in Jesus' name.

CHAPTER THREE

PLAN YOUR JOURNEY

Between you and your DREAM there will be several events. Some will be pleasant and so many not too good.
You must be able to distinguish between events that will take you up and the ones that will bring you down. Hence the need for you to plan your Journey. No plan, no movement.

Planning is the process of you going through your dream from beginning to the end even before you embark on it.

Planning is also called forethought is the process of thinking about and organizing the activities required to achieve a desired goal. It involves the ability to forecast telling what the future will be.

You are planning for something, in this case your dream life, to the very top beyond every limitation. Planning your Life's journey.

The Bible talks about God creating the world in 6 days. He could have created everything in one day, but we see God putting on proper planning.

Before he started creating anything at all, He called for light, before He created the plants, He made the Earth, before He created the animals he made the plants, before He created man, he made the plants and animals for food.

You must have a good understanding of where you are going to and how you will get there.

Stop pursuing vanity, stop chasing shadows.

Failure to prepare is the act of preparing to fail.

Those who are successful at what it is they want to do, spend a healthy amount of time planning, thinking, strategizing, and preparing in advance.

They do not wait until the moment has arrived to contemplate how they'll tackle a situation. Instead, they get as much completed and ready ahead of time, so they are freer to embrace the challenges of the moment.

Spend some time each night, and at the end of each week, reflecting on what it is you have accomplished already and what it is you want to "get done" next. Make your list, create your plan of action, and then let that ruminate in your subconscious while you sleep. And the next morning, you will be one step ahead.

Ecclesiastes 12:1 (KJV)- "Remember now thy Creator in the days of thy youth, while the evil days come not, nor the years draw nigh, when thou shalt say, I have no pleasure in them"

One asset common to all of us is TIME. The rich do not have more than the poor-The difference is what we do with our time.

Whatever you invest into your TIME, Time will pay you in multiples later on in life. If you waste it, you will reap it in POVERTY and frustration later on.

Anything or anyone that is wasting your time is wasting your life. Wasting your money- 'Time is Money'.

You are a wise person if you use your Time wisely.

If you are giving $86,400 each day, what will you do with it? Imagine the world's richest man decides he's not going to take an 11-minute space ride to the edge of space and paying $550,000,000, but rather giving you $ 31,536,000 for this year, what will you be doing with it?

Well, you already have it. Since Time is Money, God gives it to you in seconds of a Time and you have 31,536,000 s for this year. The question is 'what are you doing with it?'

You are either investing your time or merely spending it on activities or things that may be good and tension relieving but yet may not be contributing towards your major definite purpose.

You are burning it each second of the day!

Men and women that will rise to the top defiling every limitations are not people of 'que sera sera'' [what will be, will be]. These are people who know that whatever will be, will not be, if they don't do what they need to do.

To every effect there is an effort. Things don't just happen; people make them happen.

There is nothing like cheap success or promotion. Success is not about luck, chance or accident. The gentle man who wakes up and finds himself a success has not been asleep. Success is a specific effect for which there are definite causes.

Men at the top did not get there by sudden flight. You can reach the next level of your life through conscious and deliberate preparations.

Excellence is not a destination; it is a continuous journey that never ends.

Whatever level you are now, start planning and positioning yourself and take yourself to the next level.

It is only proper planning that produces proper results and proper planning requires understanding of how things work.

The power we have cannot manifest until we challenge it.

All you can do is all you can do. All you can do is enough. But ensure you do all you can do!

Success has no life until you breathe life into it.

Being exceptional is not fate, it is a decision.

The tiny things we do will not give us what we want but it will take us there.

We cannot go back and start a brand-new beginning, but we can start now and create a brand-new ending for ourselves.

Someone's opinion about you does not have to be your reality.

With proper planning it is not going to be over until you win.

TIME MANAGEMENT

Over time I have heard people talk about time management, in fact, one key knowledge area in project management is Time management. But a question we need to answer is "Can we actually manage time?" The answer is NO.

You see, managing time is beyond us as there will always be 12 months of a year, 4 weeks of a month, 7 days of a week, 24 hours of a day, 60 minutes in an hour and 60 seconds in a minute

Time is the true measure for life, its flimsy in nature, you think you have it and then realize you no longer have it. Time is fair to all. The same time allocated to you is the same allocated to the great inventors like Marie Curie "Mother of modern Physics", Maria Mayer, Thomas Edison, who alone has 1093 US patent in his name, Michael Faraday "Father of Electricity", Albert Einstein, Benjamin Franklin etc.

Our existence on earth is measured in time. On tomb stones, we see written a person's 'year of birth- year of death'. This simply tells us the time of existence, all his achievements, and accomplishments were within this time.

Joshua 13:1(NIV) - When Joshua had grown old, the LORD said to him, "You are now very old, and there are still very large areas of land to be taken over."

The question is what was he doing that he couldn't take the land as directed by God?

The man you must not meet, is the man you should have become. It's a life of regret.

We all have dreams, aspirations and hopes but those accomplishments can only be achieved when we are ready to give up something for that dream. The question is "what are you ready to give up in exchange for your dream?" Knowing fully well that you will not be having an extra time.

The same time used for pinging, chatting, face-booking, twitting, gossiping, watching television, reading novels and magazines that wouldn't improve you in any way etc., will be the same time needed for bringing that dream to pass. Life is very simple; you cannot take more than you give. For what you give is what you take! Give time to manage yourself, plan your journey.

Time begat days, day's begat years and years begat a lifetime, when a day is wasted part of a lifetime is being wasted.

Your destiny is indeed in your hands. The time is indeed ticking away, before long people will start counting down to another new year. As the new day dawns so does one gets closer to his/her time getting ready to shut down.

When a man dies, two things are likely to happen. Either he lives a vacancy, or he lives a legacy. Its either you are a Testimony or a prayer point to those you leave behind.

What will it be? How will you be remembered when your TIME shuts down?

It is easy to blame every other person for our failures but never blaming ourselves. It is your life, manage it well. Plan your life journey.

Success require that you take control of your life. It is not going to be handed to you on a platter of gold just because you dream about it.

Success demand of you a strong desire and an unwavering determination.

Michel DE Montaigne said,' No Wind favors him who has no destined Port'.

A person without a clear-cut plan in life is forever doomed to sail in circles, always frustrated, always rudderless never getting anywhere.

Planning is the end towards which effort is directed.

He who does not plan ahead, remains behind.

It is said that 'he who fails to plan, plans to fail'. So, it simply means that when you fail it was because you already planned for the failure.

The world stands aside to let anyone pass who knows where he is going. The man without purpose is like a ship without a rudder, a waif, a nothing, a no one.

You can't wonder around aimlessly in life without direction or destination and expect to get somewhere. You've got to know where you are going. Remember, success doesn't happen by accident, it happens on purpose.

It happens when you set goals to be achieved. When the set goals are achieved then you become a success.

You cannot leave your future and the development of your potential to chance or luck.

Plan for your future, you will continue to live an average mediocre hum-drum existence if you do not

When you plan, look to the future- not to the past. You cannot drive forward effectively when you are looking out the rear most frequently.

You have got to know where you are going every day.

Dwell in your dreams, refer to them, become committed to their accomplishment by setting definite time limit otherwise procrastination and delay will pilot your project, and with such commanders your dreams may never be reached.

Fear not that you shall die, rather fear that you shall stop living before you die!

AVOID PROCRASTINATION, IT'S A THIEF OF TIME

Jesus was speaking in John 9:4 (NLT)- We must quickly carry out the tasks assigned us by the one who sent us. The night is coming, and then no one can work.

Never put off for tomorrow that which you can do today. Procrastination is your greatest enemy. It has made failures out of many people. Delay will turn pregnant opportunities into hollow possibilities

Don't be a cloud because you failed to become a star.

The only thing that comes to people that procrastinate is old age. Do today what you want to postpone till tomorrow.

Begin the Job, and the work will be completed. The secret is to Start! Success and Procrastination cannot dwell together in the same room.

Success comes to the man who does today what others were thinking of doing tomorrow.

Tomorrow is the only day in the year that appeals to a lazy man. The difference between success and Failure is ACTION. Start NOW!

Remember, laziness is not the inability to work, it is the inability to complete that which was started

Follow your plans, it might not be easy but with consistency and persistence you will get there. Steven Vincent said, "Life is not lost dying, Life is lost minute by minute, day by day in all small careless ways."

Being persistent simply means you are consistent, knowing that you will get what you are going after. The most irritating man is a man that is persistent. The most annoying man is a man that is persistent. He will never accept NO as an answer.

Matthew 7:7(KJV) - "Ask, and it shall be given you; seek, and ye shall find; knock, and it shall be opened unto you... Hmm, you will agree with me here that to seek is harder than to ask, and knocking is definitely tougher than to ask or seek.

In the book of Luke 18:2-5, Jesus told the story of a widow that wanted a judge to avenge her, and the judge would not. But because of her been persistent, the Judge eventually avenged her.

Whatever you were born to be will not get to you, you have to go for it. Go and get it. Don't quit too easily. To every effect there is an effort. Things don't just happen; people make them happen.

Elijah went before God seven times to ask for rain; a lot go back after the first. Remember, Quitters never win, and winners never quit. Don't quit so easily.

You get out of life what you put into it. If we want a successful life, a life of inner peace and contentment we have to work for it, you need to push on until you push through.

Purpose is everything, the Purpose of life is a life of Purpose. Without a purpose life is meaningless, empty, and void. You are here for a purpose, discover it and live to fulfil it.

People want happiness, good health, and financial security but most people are not serious enough to plan how to get what they want out of life. They drift aimlessly like a piece of wood, wanting success to come to them or waiting for purpose to reveal itself.

Allen Weinstein says, 'Life is like boomerang, you always get back what you send out'. We all know when we flip the boomerang, according to the force we applied after it has gone through the atmosphere it returns and comes back to us.

There is no limit to how high you can go, except for the limits you place on yourself. You are actually a greater person than you think you are. This is a fact; all you have got to do is to believe it.

God have made you with great potentials for progress. All you need to do is to awake the sleeping giant within you and follow the path of progress. To unlock and unleash your full potential, you should make a habit of daily goal setting and achieving for the rest of your life

John Maxwell said,' If you don't believe that you have creative ability, you will never try to reach it. And if you are not willing to work towards reaching your potential, you will never be successful'.

THINK ON WHAT YOU HAVE TO LET GO OF TODAY TO GET TO WHERE YOU ARE GOING.

The slang amongst the young adults these days is, 'I cannot kill myself', a lot are not ready to make sacrifice for a better life. According to a lot of these young ones, Rome was not built in a day. Yes, Rome is not built in a day, but how long are you ready to give yourself to get to your destination?

The true cost of a thing is what you are ready to let go in order to get it. Think on what you have to let go today to get to your dream destination.

Before you do something, you must first be something.

The Bible says in Zechariah 4:10, for who hath despised the day of small things?

You must set goal for success and pursue it vigorously. Success requires more than wishful Thinking. A wish is just a passing thought no one takes action on it.

Remember Dreams are only Dreams until you give life to it.

Many people fail, not because they have not discovered their talents or lack of money and opportunity, they fail because they never actually planned to succeed.

In the book of Luke chapter 14:28-33, Jesus said,' For which of you, desiring to build a tower, does not first sit down and count the cost, whether he has enough to complete it? Otherwise, when he has laid a foundation and is not able to finish, all who see it begin to mock him, saying, 'This man began to build and was not able to finish.' Or what king, going out to encounter another king in war, will not sit down first and deliberate whether he is able with ten thousand to meet him who comes against him with twenty thousand? And if not, while the other is yet a great way off, he sends a delegation and asks for terms of peace. ...

Plan your future because you will live there.

In your planning, you need to have a good understanding of the TIME, where are you in time to where you need to be. You need to carry out an accurate quantifiable assessment of your situation. You need to know where you are, have a good understanding of where you are going and how to get there.

Begin to identify people who are already there and what skill set they possess. This will enable you to select your friends and also help you in improving yourself.

Proverbs 21:5(NIV) – "The plans of those who do their best lead only to having all they need, but all who are in a hurry come only to want."

Proverbs 24:27(NIV) – "Put your outdoor work in order and get your fields ready;
after that, build your house."

Proper planning entails that you go through the whole process needed from beginning to the end even though you have not started.

I know you now have a big dream, but one way of achieving that dream is to break it down into smaller achievable goals. Make these goals your steppingstones to achieving that big dream.

My prayer for you is that as you begin to plan your journey by setting your goals into motion the Power of the Almighty God will resonate with you daily and His Grace will not cease to attend to you.

CHAPTER FOUR

MIND YOUR ASSOCIATION

I would like to start this chapter with the story of Winston Churchill. Voted the Greatest Briton by the people of the United Kingdom, Winston Churchill was a two-time British Prime Minister who led his country to victory in WWII.

He was considered anything but great as a young student. But his strength in working through those early struggles and other difficulties throughout his life may have actually played a valuable role in his success.

At the age of ten while attending a boarding school in Brighton, his teachers told him he was a slow learner, forgetful, careless, unpunctual, irregular in every way and never serious. Describing himself, Churchill said, "I was, on the whole, considerably discouraged by my school days. It was not pleasant to feel ... so completely outclassed and left behind."

Failed his grade six exams. People have concluded that Churchill had dyslexia, a learning disability that affects language skills, particularly reading and spelling. As an adult, Churchill suffered recurring depression.

Whether enduring disappointing years in school, leading his nation through the hardships of war, or struggling with his own unpredictable emotions, Winston Churchill persevered. One of his greatest lessons to humankind was his ability to surround himself with people he considered far better than himself.

He was able to inspire others who faced obstacles they feared they couldn't overcome by telling them his own story of how he has come to learn from the best.

Who are your friends, who are those you surround yourself with?

You want to rise to the top, you really want to rise beyond all limits, and then it is time to re-evaluate your association.

Your network is your net worth.

The true value of having a network is not access to "things." It's access to habits and thought processes you would otherwise struggle to create on your own.

When you are surrounded by people who embody the same traits you hope to have one day, it speeds up the learning process. You inherently rise to their standard and push yourself to grow through imitation (which is actually a very good thing). Similarly, if you are surrounded by negative people, lazy people, angry and depressing people, those same traits will rub off on you.

Surround yourself with people who, in some way, are who you want to become yourself. Daniel in the Bible surrounded himself with Shadrach, Meshach and Abednego. Who are your friends?

Who you associate yourself with affects where you are going? Your company affects both your mindset and choices in life. Remember the life you are living today is a result of the decisions you made yesterday and the life you will be living tomorrow will come as a result of the decisions you will be making today and those around you now will be helping you in making those decisions.

Your associations either add to you or subtracts from you. No one associates with you and leaves you neutral.

In the book of 2 Samuel chapter 13:2-4, the Bible tells us the story of Amnon one of the sons of King David. The Bible recorded he had an inordinate affection for his sister Tamar.

He discussed this with his friend Jonadab and instead of his friend discouraging him from it, he rather encouraged him advising him wrongly. The irony of the story is that when Amnon was killed for his wrong doings it was his friend Jonadab that announced his death.

All those giving you wrong advice are waiting for your calamity.

 Whoever you give your ears to, has your heart, whoever has your heart, has your life. Ask Samson in the Bible, he refused to heed his father's warning but instead gave ears to Delilah and ended losing his eyes.

In contrast to this, when you read the book of 1Samuel 20 you find the friendship between David and Jonathan. Jonathan helped David to actualize the promise of God concerning David even though he knew it was not in the interest of his father.

Who is your friend? Either a Jonadab or a Jonathan. 1000 good friends are not enough but one bad friend is too much.

Relationships are not by force but by choice. Your friend should possess nothing less than 80% of character you desire.

Love liberally but befriend carefully.

Love is a command, but relationship is a choice. Anyone who is not going your direction should not command your association. By engagement with wrong association, you will encounter frustration. Don't pity people into friendship. Filter your relationships, categorize your relationships into outer court, inner court and the Holy place. There are some friends you meet them at the gate, there are some you meet at the living room and there should be some you can literally meet them in your bedroom these are people who you are sure have your back and will not backstab you just like the three mighty men of David in 2Samuel 23:15-16.

We all have dreams. But in order to make dreams come into reality, it takes an awful lot of determination, dedication, self-discipline, and effort.

A dream is only a dream until you give life to it!

The call of God upon our lives is the provision of God in our lives. We do not need to come to the standards of anyone else.

To copy others is to cheat yourself out of the fullness of what God has called you to be and to do. How God choses to deal with others has nothing to do with His call for us.

Galatians 6:4(NIV) – "Each one should test their own actions. Then they can take pride in themselves alone, without comparing themselves to someone else"

Your journey to accomplishing your dream on earth will not be easy, you will face challenges, oppositions, difficulties and problems.

Problems literally refers to difficulties, obstacles, hardship or something inhibiting our progress which must be dealt with. It is what stands to oppose our success as we utilize the opportunities before us. When problems arise, we do well if we act quickly to drain their momentum and move forward ourselves.

We must bear in mind that the door to opportunity swings on the hinges of opposition.

Caleb Cotton said,' Times of general calamity and confusion have and been productive of the greatest minds. The purest one is produced from the hottest furnace'.

Problems are the price of progress. The obstacles of life are intended to make us better, not bitter.

It is absolutely essential that you develop a sensible, workable philosophy for solving problems. Everyday has its problems and challenges, everyday has a daily quota of problems.

If you want to go through life without being caged under unbearable load of problem, treat each day as a unit. Do not carry yesterday to tomorrow with you. Live for today in God's strength and at the end of each day, rest in the Lord.

The advantages of Crises are Life's wake up calls. Crises are simply the call to strengthen your resolve to achieve worthwhile goals.

Bob Harrison said, 'between you and anything significant will be giant in your path'.

Oral Roberts said, "you cannot bring about renew or change without confrontation." The truth is if you like things easy you will have difficulties, if you like problems, you will succeed.

Those around you will definitely affect decisions you make in life. There are those who will never see anything good or positive around you, the very pessimistic people, while there will be some who will be optimistic. Choose wisely.

On your journey through life, you are going to face problem, trouble and difficulties. Never surrender the leadership of your life to problems, troubles and difficulties, whether they are real or imaginary. Life is full of problems. The winds of adversity never cease to blow.

Possibility thinkers are motivated by problems. They know that every problem is an opportunity for creativity. The same wind that brings adversity also carries with it seeds of creative ability, of possibilities, of Profits. Nothing is completely bad of its own. See the good in that adversity.

The true assessment of a winner is not known by how he stands in comfort and convenience, but by where he stands in challenging or confronting circumstances. God has never promised a storm free voyage across the sea but a safe landing. Life is a series of problems, either you are in one now, you are just coming out of one or you are getting ready to get into one

Robert Schuler said, "A problem free life is an illusion." Every problem has a life span. There is a time in the life span of a problem when it becomes big enough to see and yet small enough to solve.

Problems stop negative thinkers; Problems start Possibility thinkers. Problems paralyze impossibility thinkers; Problems mobilize possibility thinkers. You should not be afraid of the storm because it is the storm that actually teaches us how to sail our boats.

Success does not eliminate problems; it creates new ones. See Problems as challenges on your way to Success that must be overcome. There is no Success without a temporary failure.

Setbacks and disappointments are inevitable and unavoidable. Move forward regardless of any hardship or obstacle that may stand on your way in your life pursuit.

When you study the life of Abraham, Moses, Joseph, Peter, and Paul you see that God used the interjection of

a major problems to lead the heroes of faith to move beyond mediocrity to a life at the maximum.

The Pole vaulter cannot be certain that he has jumped as
high as he possibly can until he knocks the bar down.
Keep raising your goal until you have reached your
peak.

The Gem cannot be polished without friction, no man is
perfected without trial.

Deuteronomy 32:11-12(NIV) – "Like an eagle that stirs
up its nest
and hovers over its young, that spreads its wings to
catch them
and carries them aloft.[12] The LORD alone led him;
no foreign god was with him. So, the LORD alone did
lead him, and there was no strange god with him."

If God cushioned your every blow, you would never
learn to grow.

The pushing into Crises is His supreme act of Love, a
kind of that of mother eagle that pushes her young from
the nest to force them to fly.

Don't be a dove if you were born an eagle. Experience
God's altitude for your life.

Don't live your Life on Other People's Opinion:

To fulfill your dream, in life you will usually have to
swim upstream against the tide of popular opinion.
These opinions could be from friends and family mem-

bers. Opposition is the proof that you are swimming not floating.

The only way to avoid criticism is to do nothing and be nothing!

Psalms 107:23-30(KJV): -They that go down to the sea in ships, that do business in great waters; these see the works of the LORD, and his wonders in the deep.

For He commandeth, and raiseth the stormy wind, which lifteth up the waves thereof.

They mount up to the heaven, they go down again to the depths: their soul is melted because of trouble.

They reel to and from, and stagger like a drunken man, and are at their wit's end.

Then they cry unto the LORD in their trouble, and He bringeth them out of their distresses.

He maketh the storm a calm, so that the waves thereof are still.

Then are they glad because they be quiet; so, He bringeth them unto their desired haven."

Compromised Vision always kill creative ability, because a Vision that is attempted outside God's guidelines cannot reveal His purpose. Take your dream and be willing to die for it.

We are not called to respond to criticism, we are called to respond to God. It is the voice of God that we must obey.

Many dreams are killed by laughter and ridicule, but your dream doesn't have to die. Dare to be different. Accomplish Something!

Remember: If a thousand persons say something foolish, it is still foolish. Truth is never dependent upon consensus of opinion.

Who has the deciding vote to kill your dream? Well, it is only you!

Martin Luther King Jr, said "No one can take a ride on your back unless you bend."

Do not worry about public opinion. Only be concerned about your commander's opinion. If you fear God, there is no need to fear anything else.

Time changes everything, but you change everything by what you do with the Time you have. If you wait for the perfect conditions, you will never get anything done. Time waits for no one. All that you do with Time today determines your future tomorrow.

Gain control over your time, and you will gain control over your life. Your Time is precious as your life. To waste your Time is to waste your Life, but to master your time is to master your life.

Time wasted is irreversible. The wise man makes the best of his time.

Avoid Time wasters! Yes, some persons are just there to waste your time. They are going nowhere, and they know it. All they want to do is waste your time.

Ronald Wilson Raegan was the 40th president of the United States. A former Hollywood movie actor. When he was elected as president many expected him to fail but he didn't. A reporter once asked him what the secret of his success was. His answer was, '"Surround yourself with the best people you can find, delegate authority, and don't interfere as long as the policy you've decided upon is being carried out."

Who are those you surround yourself with?

PEOPLE TO AVOID

1. TIME WASTERS: Genesis 24:55-56(NIV) - But her brother and her mother said, "Let the girl stay with us a few days, at least ten. Then she may go." [56] But he said to them, "Do not make me stay any more days, since the Lord has made my way go well. Send me away so I may go to my boss."

These are the people that want you around because of what they are getting from you. They would want you around them in other to keep you away from the promises of God in your life.

2. DREAM KILLERS: 1 Kings 13:11-24; Genesis 37:23-28

These are people that will not rest until they kill your dream. In the book of 1 Kings 13:11-24, the Bible recorded that the old prophet went after the young prophet brought him home and was able to convince him in contradiction to God's injunctions for him. He did not rest until the young prophet died. Josephs brothers were also like that, they wanted him dead to ensure that his dreams never actualized.

3. DESTINY MOCKERS: Nehemiah 4:1-6

These are people that will mock and ridicule you. They will say all manner of evil concerning you. Their intention is to discourage you from fulfilling your dream. A lot of Dreams have been killed by laughter and ridicule, don't let them kill your Dream.

4. DESTINY BORROWERS: Genesis 30:27(NIV) - But Laban said to him, "If now it pleases you, stay with me. I have learned that the Lord has brought good to me because of you." These are people who just want you around to prosper at your expense.

I heard the story of this young man working for this elderly man in his company. One day the young man decided to resign and start off his company. The elderly man tried discouraging him and promised to double his salary.

The young man insisted he was living. The elderly man agreed to pay him four times what he was earning. The young man was surprised. So, he asked the elderly man,' so you know am worth 4 times what am been paid all this while and you never increased my salaries?'

To his surprise the elderly man told him, 'Is it not written in your Bible, ask and it shall be given. You have never asked.

Well, the young man left, started his own company and was a Success.

Just like this elderly employer, Laban was prospered at the detriment of Jacob hence the reason why he wanted him to continue to stay with him.

5. DESTINY EXCHANGERS: 1Kings 3:16-23

These are people that will take what belongs to A and give it to B. They could be parents, relatives or friends. They are not happy you are the one with the big achievements, they wish it was your younger ones or other persons but not you.

PEOPLE THAT YOU NEED

1. DESTINY POINTERS: 1King 1:1-12; 1King 19:19

   These are people that will wake you up to your destiny in life. They will wake you up to things you need to know and do in life to fulfil your destiny.

   Destiny pointers only lead you, after which they disappear. They don't contend with you. When a man doesn't meet his destiny pointers that man will miss out in the radar of life. Just like a plane lost from the radar is in trouble.

   Isaiah 30:21(NIV)- Whether you turn to the right or to the left, your ears will hear a voice behind you, saying, "This is the way; walk in it."

2. DESTINY SUPPORTERS: Acts 9:26-27. 1king 1:12

   It is not enough for a man to start off, you need someone to guide you and water your destiny in order for you to get there.

   You need a Nathan. You need a Barnabas

People that will assist you on your way in life. They will support you, back you up and encourage you as you walk in the path of life.

3. DESTINY HELPERS: Exodus 17:11-12

> As long as Moses held up his hands, the Israelites were winning, but whenever he lowered his hands, the Amalekites were winning. [12] When Moses' hands grew tired, they took a stone and put it under him, and he sat on it. Aaron and Hur held his hands up—one on one side, one on the other—so that his hands remained steady till sunset.

> In life, there's no explanation for failure. No matter the story, all people want to hear is how you succeeded. Destiny helpers are people that will emerge when it seems all hope is lost.

> As a child of God you are not expected to live a regular life. If men live a normal life, you should live a miraculous life.

> Associate with successful people, people you can learn from. If you are going to learn how to fly, fly with the eagles. You cannot be scratching with the chickens.

1 John 4:4(NIV) - You, dear children, are from God and have overcome them, because the one who is in you is greater than the one who is in the world.

We cannot conclude this chapter without asking that you make God your friend. For without him we are nothing.

Psalms 32:8(NIV)- I will instruct you and teach you in the way you should go; I will counsel you with my loving eye on you.

Whenever you are with people, is either you are influencing them or being influenced by them.

Choose your friends wisely!

CHAPTER FIVE

IMPROVE YOURSELF

In the 1950s a baby girl was born to a young impoverished teenage mother in rural Mississippi. This young girl grew up poor, with no formal education, at a young age she suffered abuse and at age 9 she decided to run away from home, but at age 13 she was pregnant.

After she lost her first child at 14, she decided to move to Tennessee to live with her father and there she turned the table on her disastrous upbringing. She began to excel in school by studying really hard. She did well in speech and debate. She even won a state beauty pageant. While in school she worked part-time reading news for a local radio station. She studied so hard that she ended earning a scholarship to the college at Tennessee State.

In college, this wounded girl became a powerhouse of a woman. She majored in communications and landed her first post-graduation job at a Nashville station. That turned into a bigger gig with an ABC affiliate in Baltimore. Soon after that, she was hired as a primetime news co-anchor, an incredible feat considering she was a young, black woman in an era where old, white men made and enforced all the rules.

In her career as a broadcaster, there were moments she considered herself a failure but, in such instances, she just picks herself up, dust herself and moved on.

According to her, her unique combination of empathy, determination, and the ability to keep moving forward when all else had fallen apart and her ability to excel in business while not being business-oriented was a marvel.

That young girl was Oprah Winfrey. Her show, the Oprah show was an American daytime Syndicated talk show that aired nationwide for 25 years. It was and remains the highest rated daytime talk show in American television history.

Moral of the story? Have passion, believe in your dreams, believe in yourself even when no one else does, and keep going when hope is lost. Don't be afraid to fail, always work on yourself to improve yourself.

You see, growth is a process not an event. We develop day by day. It is a process it evolves over time. Secrete to development is Practice, Practice and Practice.

Success occurs when your preparation meets opportunity. When you are not prepared when your opportunity comes you will look like a fool.

Growth is like a rubber band it stops when you lose the tension between where you are and where you could be.

True growth begins at the end of your comfort zone.

Your growth in life must be intentional. Your improvement must be intentional, no one improves by accident. How much you grow will determine how far you will go.

You must grow up. If you jump up, you will come down. If you grow up, you will remain there. Growing up is an option, getting old is compulsory. Are you getting old or growing up?

Proverbs 19:2(NIV)- Desire without knowledge is not good—
how much more will hasty feet miss the way!

A lot do not take up the responsibility of developing themselves as a result they only get by instead of them getting better.

Improving yourself is not a daydream, it requires a lot of discipline. Discipline keeps you going. You are exactly where you should be giving all that you have done to get here.

The successful person has the habit of doing the things that failures don't like to do. The successful person doesn't like to do them either, but his dislike is subordinated to the strength of his purpose.

Some things will not happen quickly, suddenly, as soon as, immediately or now. One of such things is your growth in life. Your Growth is a whole life process.

An improved economy in your country does not automatically translate to an improved life for you if you do not take advantage of the improvement policies and platforms put in place by the Government.

Many of us have made costly mistakes in the past. Trusted wrong people, offended many people, and indulged in acts that brought shame, reproach, disgrace or embarrassment. We have been criticized, condemned, treated without respect and the stigma of our past errors won't just let us be.

So, we have decided to chill let life and circumstances lead us on. We have resolved not to be too involved even in matters of our own lives.

My advice is don't be a prisoner to yesterday. Yesterday's the past, tomorrow is the future, but today is a gift. That is why it's called the present.

You are and can be better than this. What you don't know is that the hurt and bitter experiences of the past released in you certain strengths and psychological advantages you would not have acquired if you never experienced that past.

You want to be a diamond, then be ready to be cut like a diamond. If you think this you, will take you to your next level then you are joking. You must be a tougher, stronger more determined you to get to the next level. Do not let the noise of other people's opinion to drown your own inner voice.

In production it is said that every product is preceded by a need. So, the purpose of every product is to meet an already existed need. God created you for a purpose, He created you to fill a gap somewhere.

Jeremiah 1:5(NIV)- "Before I formed you in the womb I knew you, before you were born I set you apart; I appointed you as a prophet to the nations."
Your value and importance in life will be to the degree

of how well you fulfill your purpose. Purpose is the key word to life, without purpose, life is not complete.

We all have dreams. But in order to make dreams come into reality, it takes an awful lot of determination, dedication, self-discipline, and effort.

Find your 'why' and you will find your way to grow. Good enough is truly the motto of the defeated. Growing is stretching, make it a lifestyle

You must deliver result, be competent at what you are doing. Stop the excuses, excuses are the building blocks for a house of failure. There is no room for excuses.

A lot do not take up the responsibility of developing themselves as a result they only get by instead of them getting better. Growth doesn't just happen- it is not a natural process. You must go out of your comfort zone to grow.

No one improves by accident we have to do it intentionally.

Stop comparing yourself to others, it's a useless thing to do. There will always be people better than you and there are also people you are better than.

Instead of comparing yourself with others learn from them if they are ahead of you and move on growing consistently.

Do you know what you need to improve on? Do you know how you need to improve yourself?

Make your greatest FEAR, achieving Mediocrity.

Remember for you to grow is for you to stretch, and very few people will stretch.

People will always prefer the status quo which ultimately leads to destruction. Break the status quo.

Seek Knowledge, improve your understanding. Understanding is you knowing how things work-it is you having good judgment. Do you really know how things work?

Ask questions, be identified with people who know. You can't afford to navigate life from the perspective of ignorance. Read books, listen to News, and look out for opportunities. The difference between the rich and the poor is information. The line between where you are and where you need to be is called knowledge.

If there is anything that pricks the heart of God is seeing His children living below His standard for them. It is God's will that you prosper, it is His will that you succeed in life, it is His will that all that you lay your hand upon prospers.

Psalms 1:3 (NIV)- That person is like a tree planted by streams of water, which yields its fruit in season and whose leaf does not wither— whatever they do prospers.

The only thing holding you from getting to your next level is you. If you have all it takes to attain your next level, the truth is, you should have been there, but you are not because there are some things you need to know, there are some skills to be acquired.

Abraham Lincoln said,' the things I want to know are in books; my best friend is the man who'll get me a book I haven't read'.

How much do you really know? What is your level of knowledge on that subject matter?

Study to know, that's what the Bible says in 2Timothy 2:15(KJV) - Study to shew thyself approved unto God, a workman that needeth not to be ashamed, rightly dividing the word of truth.

What is the worth of the content in your head? If we decide to evaluate the content in your head, how much will it cost? What will people be willing to pay for it?

You want to excel in life, learn to read. Paul was inspired yet calls for books to read. 2Timothy 4:13(AMP)- When you come bring the coat that I left at Troas with Carpus, and the books, especially the parchments.

There is nothing like cheap success or promotion. Success is not about luck, chance, or accident. The gentle man who wakes up and finds himself a success has not been asleep. Success is a specific effect for which there are definite causes. Men at the top did not get there by sudden flight. You can reach the next level of your life through conscious and deliberate preparations.

Excellence is not a destination; it is a continuous journey that never ends. Whatever level you are now, position yourself and take yourself to the next level.

What is understanding? It is knowing how things work. Proverbs 17:27, tells us the man that has understanding has an excellent spirit. No wonder Daniel excelled and was preferred even in a foreign land.

Even God cannot deliver a man who is ignorant. Ignorance is not an excuse. Hosea 4:6a (NIV)- my people are destroyed from lack of knowledge.

Study to know how things really works. In your career, in that business venture whatever it is you desire to go into, have a good understanding of how things work. If a man lacks understanding in a thing, he becomes incompetent in that thing.

Twice Jesus wept in the Bible, once was because his friend died the second was at the ignorance of the people. Luke 19:41-42 (KJV)-.

"As he approached Jerusalem and saw the city, he wept over it [42] and said, "If you, even you, had only known on this day what would bring you peace—but now it is hidden from your eyes."

Do you really know? Partial knowledge is worse, have a full knowledge of how things really work.

John 8:32 says you shall know the truth and the truth will make you free. It is the truth you really know and apply that sets you free.

The power we have can't manifest until we challenge it.

All you can do is all you can do. All you can do is enough. But ensure you do all you can do, and one way in doing all you can do is making yourself a better person by developing yourself.

Success has no life until you breathe life into it.

Being exceptional is not fate, it's a decision.

Tiny things will not give you what you want but it will take you there.

You cannot go back and start a brand-new beginning, but you can start now and create a brand-new ending for yourself.

If you want to be successful and rise above every limitation, you're going to have to say NO a lot more than you say YES. Want to go hang out at the bar? Want to post up for the afternoon and watch football? Want to take an extended vacation? Want to watch TV? None of these things are bad in themselves, but if you still haven't made your dream come true, then realize that every time you say YES to what someone else wants you to do, you are saying NO to whatever it is you truly want to do.

It's a judgment call, and one a lot (and I mean a lot) of people struggle with. Successful people are very conscious of how they spend their time.

Both in terms of time and money, successful people see life through a lens of investment.

The majority of people don't invest; they spend. They spend the money they earn. They spend their time with people they don't really like, doing things they don't really enjoy. They spend and spend and then wake up one morning wondering why their life is the way it is.

Warren Buffet said,' If you buy things, you do not need, soon you will have to sell things you need'.

Do not save what is left after spending, spend what is left after saving.

Successful people, on the other hand, invest. They are conscious of how they spend their time and invest it toward their goals. They invest their money in creating additional revenue streams, not owning depreciating assets. They invest in themselves, taking courses, exposing themselves to worthwhile attractions, feeding their interests.

Investing over time is what ultimately creates wealth, both financially and in terms of knowledge. How much is your phone, your shoes, your suit etc.? I asked earlier, 'what is the value of the content in your head?' Do you have an answer now? Do something every day to become a better you.

Education does not cost. - It pays.

The shortest distance between where you are and where you could be is-knowledge. The difference between HERE where you are now and THERE which you need to be is letter T which is time. You will get there if you do what you ought to do. Improve yourself.

Stop spending more money on outside of your head than what is inside. (Make-ups, hair do, haircuts, shampoo, the eye lashes, eye liner, eye shadow, mascara, lip stick, concealer, blusher, powder, plastic surgery, Brazilian hair etc.)

There are a lot of people in the world who believe that life operates the same way as formal education. They go to college, get their diploma, start working at a big company, and then just assume that over time their years spent there will carry them up the ladder to a nice and comfortable position (just as you rise from fresh-man to senior).

Unfortunately, there are situations that reward the fundamental metric of time, and people can climb the ladder of "success" by simply staying the course. But the truth is, those are not the ones who end up becoming thought leaders, innovators, industry experts, or even accomplished creators. Because to do that, you have to actively be studying your craft in ways that does not happen by simply clocking in at 8 and clocking out at 5.

Proverbs 22:29(NIV) - Do you see someone skilled in their work? They will serve before kings; they will not serve before officials of low rank.

Successful people don't separate their job and their "personal life." Their job is their passion, and their passion is their craft. They study their craft relentlessly because it is part of who they are. It is not dependent upon time. It is merely a reflection of their own curiosity.

You won't be rewarded for doing what you're meant to do, you only get a salary for that!

You're only rewarded for going an extra mile, performing beyond expectations. To be successful in life you must be observant, proactive and willing to do more, think more, a more holistic perspective and go beyond the call of duty. May you be blessed with a better perspective to your work this year? Greater life needs this mentality of going an extra mile, as husband's, mothers, children...let's go an extra mile in all our endeavor...

MAKE YOUR PERSONAL DEVELOPMENT A TOP PRIORITY

Your personal development is the key to your advancement in life. The height to which you will rise will be determined by the degree to which you develop yourself. It is rather surprising that men are anxious to improve their circumstances but unwilling to improve themselves. They therefore remain bound to same level year after year, month after month, week after week.

Martin Luther King Jnr said, 'If a man can't fly, let him run, if he can't run let him walk, if he can't walk let him crawl, but by all means let him move.'

The Bible said,' Of the increase of his Kingdom there shall be no end' (Isaiah 9:7). God expects us to be better persons with each passing day.

You must become someone that you have never been before to get a position higher than you are now. You must continually work hard on yourself and never stop because the major key to your future is you.

ACQUIRE KNOWLEDGE

Bishop Oyedepo said, 'to be informed is to be transformed, and to be uninformed is to be deformed'.

My friend give yourself to study, read books. A friend told me, books are the quietest and most constant of friends, they are the most accessible and wisest of counsellors and most patient of teachers.

Proverbs 21:16(KJV) - The man that wandereth out of the way of understanding shall remain in the congregation of the dead. This simply tells us that a man that fails to improve himself is better off dead.

DEVELOP SKILLS

Many people are backward and mediocre in their work, career, or profession because they have not given appropriate value to skill. Anointing is no substitute for skills, Prayers are no substitutes either. It is important to determine where you are headed and what skills you need to get there. Ecclesiastes 9:10(NIV)- Whatever your hand finds to do, do it with all your might, for in the realm of the dead, where you are going, there is neither working nor planning nor knowledge nor wisdom.

Proverbs 22:29(NIV) - Do you see someone skilled in their work? They will serve before kings; they will not serve before officials of low rank.

George Orwell said, 'we say that a man's dead when his heart stops and not before. It seems a bit arbitrary. After all, parts of your body don't stop working-hair goes on growing for years, for instance. Perhaps a man really dies when his brain stops, when he loses the power to take in a new idea."

Henry Ford says, 'Anyone who stops learning is old whether at twenty or eighty

Anyone who keeps learning stays young. The greatest thing in life is to keep your mind young'.

Your destiny is indeed in your hands, you are the manager of your life. It is time you begin to take full responsibility of your life and stop blaming everyone else.

Become a student of life, a student of Ideas, insight, truth, wisdom. You must give value to yourself. Remember, it is only the man that creates value that is said to be valuable.

In the face of necessity skill is appreciated than position. The seat of knowledge is the head, the seat of Wisdom is the Heart. Until you move what you have in your head to your heart knowledge is useless. When you are armed with wisdom you rule every aspect of life.

Grow and stretch beyond your present limit my friend, have at the back of your mind: He who fails to innovate will eventually evaporate and anything you don't use eventually decays in your hand.

CHAPTER SIX

SAY IT

Today Albert Einstein is celebrated and considered one of the greatest minds of our time. Story has it that as a young boy his parents considered him a big liability. At age 4 he couldn't speak, leant to read at age 7. He came back from school one day with a letter the school had asked him to give to his mother. As he hands her the letter, he asks she read him the content. The mother reads the letter and tells him the school said he is far too intelligent to attend, and they were asking for him not to return.

His mother had experience as an educator, so she elected to home school Albert.

As the story goes, years later after he had gained name and fame, he went back to his family house, Albert found the letter handed to him years past by his elementary school teacher and read it and this is what it really said. Dear Mrs Einstein. We the board feel Albert Einstein is a distraction and is not mentally equipped to handle school like most of the other children. We are expelling him, and he is not to return.

Why did the mother tell him a different story as a child? It was simply because she understood the power of WORDS. She knew words are like seeds, and when they grow, they will become the young boy's reality.

She understood the damage such words would have on the young boy and decided to create a different reality for him. Knowing that that was what he was then, but that was not who he was. She saw greatness in him, and so she decided to create a different world for him.

Just like Mrs Einstein, I want you to realize this fundamental truth that the words you speak are not just words, they are seed. And like every seed they have the potential to grow. When your words grow, they become your reality.

God is not only interested in just hearing what we say, He is equally interested in ensuring that we get what we say.

If you are satisfied with your life Heaven is also satisfied. Whatever you allow on earth, will be allowed in Heaven the Bible said. Matthew 18:18(NIV)- "Truly I tell you, whatever you bind on earth will be[a] bound in heaven, and whatever you loose on earth will be[b] loosed in heaven.

Matthew 16:19(NIV)- I will give you the keys of the kingdom of heaven; whatever you bind on earth will be[a] bound in heaven, and whatever you loose on earth will be[b] loosed in heaven."

Listen, a closed mouth is a closed Destiny. Any man who cannot speak cannot alter the direction of his life.

In the book of 1Chronicles 4:9-10, we were told the story of a young man named Jabez: [9] Jabez was more honourable than his brothers. His mother had named him Jabez,[a] saying, "I gave birth to him in pain." [10] Jabez cried out to the God of Israel, "Oh, that you would bless me and enlarge my territory! Let your hand be with me and keep me from harm so that I will be free from pain." And God granted his request.

The Bible recorded that the mother called him Jabez-Jabez meaning," He makes sorrow", "he causes sorrow". She named him based on the circumstances surrounding his birth. Whenever I read this scripture, I just wonder where his father was. May be his father died at his birth, may be the father left the mother, or he was a product of a rape, the Bible never told us anything about his father but whatever the case, we know it was not pleasant, and the reason why the mother called him by that name. It seems a cruel, insensitive, and selfish choice – a mother who deliberately crippled her son's destiny with a name which had nothing to do with him, and everything to do with her.

But the Bible rightly stated this young man altered the cause of his life by crying out to God and telling Him exactly what he wanted to happen in his life. At the end he became more honourable than his brethren.

Numbers 14:28(KJV) - Say unto them, as truly as I live, saith the LORD, as ye have spoken in mine ears, so will I do to you:

It is not what you see that matters, it's what you want to see that counts.

In Genesis 1:1-3, the Bible recorded that the world was without form and void, darkness was upon the face of the deep. What did God do? God spoke. He called for the light, and He saw light.

This is what FAITH is all about. Being able to say it, when you have not seen it. In contrast, a natural man wants to see it before he says it. Romans 4:17, says He calls those things that are not as if they are.

There are times we are faced with situations where it seems there is no Hope, everything looks gloomy, No Form, No Shape, everything looks so dark.

That was the same situation God was faced with. God spoke.

He did not complain, He was not confused, He was not depressed, and He didn't call a friend to complain so they can sympathize with Him. All He did was to speak to the situation.

What are you speaking concerning your situation? Yes, you have identified a challenge to your dream, you see a problem, you have encountered some obstacles, some things are not going as planned, and so what?

Remember, every limitation you see today, some persons some time have faced same and did overcome it. If they did overcome it, so can you. What are you saying concerning it?

Jesus was speaking in Mark 11:23(NIV)- "Truly I tell you, if anyone says to this mountain, 'Go, throw yourself into the sea,' and does not doubt in their heart but believes that what they say will happen, it will be done for them.

God used His word to create order. The world was without form and void, darkness was upon the Earth. In the midst of the chaos, He spoke, He called for light. What do you use your words for?

Imagine yourself as a god, well stop imagining because he rightly called you a god. Psalms 82:6(NIV) - "I said, 'you are "gods"; you are all sons of the Most High.'

He showed we are gods and co-creators with Him in the book of Genesis chapter 2:19, when He asked Man to give names to everything that He had created. Normally, it is the creator, inventor or the discoverer of a thing that gives name to his creation, his invention, his discovery but here we see God asking man to name His creation as a co-creator.

So as gods, our words ought to be creative. We need to use our words to restore order in the midst of chaos.

The words from your mouth are not just mere words, the Bible says that they are POWER. 1Corinthians 4:20 said, for the kingdom of God is not in word, but in power.

So just in the same way the Bible told us that the word of God does not go out in vain, i.e., Isaiah 55:11(ERV)-
In the same way, my words leave my mouth,
 and they don't come back without results.
My words make the things that I want to happen, HAPPEN.
 They succeed in doing what I send them to do.

You need to start seeing yourself in this same light. That whatever you say will definitely come to pass. It will HAPPEN.

The book of Numbers 23:19, says,' God is not a man; he will not lie. God is not a human being; his decisions will not change. If he says he will do something, then he will do it.

If he makes a promise, then he will do what he promised.

God works with us based on His word. He will never contradict His word, and so expects us to come to Him on the bases of His word.

So, whenever you need to speak, if the words are not in line with the word of God, ZIP it UP. Don't Say IT!

You cannot speak evil of yourself and expect to have a good life. You want to know how and where you will be in 5 years' time. Then start listening to what you are saying about yourself today.

The book of Proverbs 18: 21(KJV)-Death and life are in the power of the tongue: and they that love it shall eat the fruit thereof.

Proverbs 13: 2a, (KJV), "A man shall eat good by the fruit of his mouth:

Proverbs 6:2, (KJV), "Thou art snared with the words of thy mouth, thou art taken with the words of thy mouth."

Matthew 12:3, (KJV), "For by thy words thou shalt be justified, and by thy words thou shalt be condemned."

From the scriptures above, it is evident that God not only hears us but ensures that we get exactly what we say. If you go about saying things like "Am not going to make it: Then you cannot make it. Am so tired, then you will never be strong. Am not good enough, then someone else will always be preferred to you. This sickness will kill me, of course is just a matter of time, it will.

And in the same vein if you start saying things like "I'm strong, strength starts coming your way: I'm well, and healing comes for you: I'm rich and riches, prosperity comes for you: I'm blessed, and you start seeing God's blessings coming after you:"

I cannot fail, am fearfully and wonderfully made. I cannot die, I will live to declare the good works of the Lord in the land of the living.

So as the scripture says in Proverbs 18:21, (KJV), "Death and life are in the power of the tongue: and they that love it shall eat the fruit thereof." It simply means that whatever you say, you have. Whatever you say you automatically gives an invitation. So do yourself some good, stop inviting the negatives into your life. Start blessing your future with your words. You want to change your world? Then change your word. Why? Because your word is your world. You cannot separate a man from his word!

In the book of Numbers 13:25-33, the Bible talks about Moses sending 12 spies to spy the Promised Land. We remember the names of 2 of them so well, Joshua and Caleb but forget about the other 10. Most Bible students don't remember this other 10 because while Joshua and Caleb brought a good report, telling the people that they are able to go up and take the country, the other ten brought an evil report. They said they were not able, that they were like grasshoppers both in their eyes and in the eyes of the people.

They were spies, their identities were supposed to be hidden, how were the people they were to spy on able to see they were grasshoppers? Yes, they exaggerated. And God promised them just as they have spoken, they will get. And yes, they got what they said, everyone from 20 years above died in the wilderness. Why? Because of their word.

In the book of Jeremiah chapter 1:6-7, we see God giving a warning to the prophet Jeremiah never to say he was a child, even though he was indeed a child.

In the book of Luke chapter 1 we see the encounter between Zacharias the Priest and the angel Gabriel. The angel told him he and his wife, were going to have a son, but he saw it as been impossible, he sees the news coming rather too late and told the angel he and his wife were old. The angel told him he was going to be dumb and not able to speak until the child was born.

The angel knew if he went out saying such words, he would end up delaying the plans of God. No matter the promise that God has made concerning you, if you go speaking contrary to His word you will end up stopping what He has destined for you.

What is your story? It is your story that is making you sick and holding you down. You have given so much power to your story that your story now justifies your condition.

Remember the man at the pool of Bethesda for 38 years in the book of John chapter 5, Jesus asked him, would thou be made whole? He only complained, only if I had someone. A lot of us have been complaining just like that.

Nobody to help me, I did not have quality education, my parents, my siblings, my stepmother, my stepfather. I was raped, I am an orphan. Please fix your story.

Go ask Oprah Winfrey. Steve Jobs, Bill Gates, Winston Churchill, Jessica Cox, Nick Vujicic, etc. they all changed their stories.

This was what happened to the woman with the issue of blood in Mark 5:25-34.

Everybody else said she was going to die. The doctors, her family members, neighbors, church members, and coworkers you name it. She was the only one with a different story.

If only I can touch the hem of his garment, I will be made whole.

She changed her story. She said it again and again, over and over.

When you repeat a new story, you delete an old story. You cannot have a new story until you reset your mind. You need to renew your mind through the word of God as we had already discussed in chapter one.

Romans 12:2 (NIV), - Do not conform to the pattern of this world but be transformed by the renewing of your mind. Then you will be able to test and approve what God's will is—his good, pleasing and perfect will.

What healed her was her story. She changed her story, so her circumstance changed.

The question for you today is what will you declare for yourself? Victory or defeat? Life or death? Failure or Success? Health or Sickness?

Jeremiah 1:12, said, 'then said the LORD unto me, thou hast well seen: for I will hasten my word to perform it.

This scripture simply tells us that God will do anything to see that His word comes to pass.

Joshua 6:10(KJV), 'And Joshua had commanded the people, saying, Ye shall not shout, nor make any noise with your voice, neither shall any word proceed out of your mouth, until the day I bid you shout; then shall ye shout'.

No matter what God said concerning you, you can alter it by saying contrary. Joshua knew this and so instructed the people not to say anything.

Job 22:28(KJV),'thou shalt also decree a thing, and it shall be established unto thee: and the light shall shine upon thy ways'.

So, stop focusing on your flaws. You have enough in life against you already, don't be against yourself. When you start saying beautiful things about yourself, your inner man comes alive. You start carrying yourself with a form of dignity. Beauty is being what God made you to be with pride. Remember you are his masterpiece and there will never be another you.

Don't use your words to curse your future but rather use it to bless your future. The Bible says "let the weak say I am strong. Notice just the opposite of how they feel. In the same vein let the poor say am rich.

What you keep saying comes looking for you. Don't be against yourself. You already have so much against you in life, don't add to the list. Don't say another negative word against yourself.

It is just as wrong criticizing yourself as criticizing someone else. You need to change what you are saying about yourself.

When you get up in the morning, look yourself in the mirror and say.

Good morning you beautiful thing.

The woman with the issue of blood was saying something positive to herself right in the midst of the difficulty.

This is my day, this is my time, and this is my moment.

You are constantly moving towards what you are constantly saying.

Remember you will soon see what you are saying.

Jesus was speaking in the book of Matthew 15:18(KJV), 'but those things which proceed out of the mouth come forth from the heart; and they defile the man.

In Chapter 1 of this book, we established the fact that your mind is a very powerful tool. Also know that your tongue is equally as powerful. In the book of Matthew 18:18(ERV) Jesus said,' [I] assure you *and* most solemnly say to you, whatever you bind [forbid, declare to be improper and unlawful] on earth shall have [already] been bound in heaven, and whatever you loose [permit, declare lawful] on earth shall have [already] been loosed in heaven.

James 3:3-6; when we put bits into the mouths of horses to make them obey us, we can turn the whole animal. Or take ships as an example. Although they are so large and are driven by strong winds, they are steered by a very small rudder wherever the pilot wants to go. Likewise, the tongue is a small part of the body, but it makes great boasts. Consider what a great forest is set on fire by a small spark. The tongue also is a fire, a world of evil among the parts of the body. It corrupts the whole body, sets the whole course of one's life on fire, and is itself set on fire by hell."

So, you can change your world by changing your words. Remember death and life are in the power of the tongue.

Write His words down, read it to yourself aloud.

Say it, don't stop saying it. Say it until it sinks into your subconscious.

Psalms 33:9 (NIV)- For he spoke, and it came to be
  he commanded, and it stood firm.

God is irrevocably committed to His word. The word of God is the comfort that we get in the mist of trouble. When God steps in miracles takes place.

God is still in the making your dream come through business, He is still in the get your life together business.

You can't put any limitations on God, if you just get out of the way, He will do miraculous things all the time.

Say it, in the place of prayer. Don't forget to pray. Don't be ashamed to pray. Don't be too proud to pray. Prayer changes things, prayer changes people.

Psalms 103:20(NIV) - Praise the LORD, you his angels,
  you mighty ones who do his bidding,
  who obey his word.

The voice might be yours but let the word be His!

Keep saying it, don't stop saying it. Don't stop talking it. You hold on to it until the day dawn.

Read it aloud to yourself. As you do this, very soon it will become your reality and you will go on to become what He created you to be.

CHAPTER SEVEN

WORK IT

The primary difference between a success and a failure is "ACTION" and Complacency is the enemy of progress.

For you getting this far, I want to believe that you are serious about actualizing your dream. I also want to believe that by now you have broken that dream into achievable goals, and you already set out a plan on how to achieve each goal. Now we come to the point where we get to know those who are really determined to succeed.

Anyone that has gotten to this level has an aspiration, but aspiration without inspiration leads to frustration.

Thomas Edison said, "Vision without Execution is Hallucination".

Hallucination is a sensory perception of something that does not exit, often arising from disorder of the nervous system. It's simply a Delusion.

Men and women who accomplish tremendous deeds in life are intensely action oriented. They are moving all the time. They are always busy. If they have an idea, they take actions on it immediately. They know that an idea is always open to others, and it will always benefits the one who takes immediate action.

You have great dreams, but what are you doing concerning it now? You are waiting for the right moment to start off. Well, just to let you know, you are not the only one with that dream. Start now, no matter how small. Remember the tiny things will not give us what we desire, but it will definitely take us there.

Laziness is not the inability to do work but the inability to complete what was started. You have started, the question is," will you be able to finish it?"

Lazy People are not accountable for their actions: Lazy people point the finger at others and make excuses for why things didn't happen. Successful people own up to the weight of their actions and take accountability for their own shortcomings.

This is a habit and a mindset, and one that takes years to cultivate properly. To truly be successful, you have to be extremely self-aware and willing to question the reality you are living. If things are amiss or not going the way you want them to, you cannot point at others and blame them for your unhappiness, dissatisfaction, etc. You have to own up and admit that you created your reality and nobody else.

Lazy people want others to believe in them before they believe in themselves.

Successful people, on the other hand, believe in themselves against all odds, often times long before anyone else does. To be successful, this is a must. You cannot expect others to support and believe in something that you cannot even tap into. Don't let people's doubt make you doubt yourself. It has to come from you before it can come from anyone else.

In life we all have suffered a defeat, but how you deal with the defeat is as important as how you deal with your victory. To do this, however, you must take considerable time to understand, to know, and nurture yourself. It's tough work, but it's foundational work, and is often what makes the difference between building something that lasts and instead hoping for short-lasting approval.

Believe in yourself. That's where it all starts. E.g., Steve Jobs, Bill gate, Bill Clinton, Albert Einstein, Oprah Winfrey, Barak Obama, etc. They all believed in themselves, and they worked hard for their success.

People's lack of Faith in you, should not affect yours. People will trust you as long as you trust yourself. The confidence doesn't come from what people think about you, it comes from within yourself.

Back home in Nigeria in my small-town Abbi in Delta state, the story is told of a young prince the only son of the king. He had a friend who was the son of a poor farmer in the village.

One day both of them were playing and somehow, they got lost and found themselves in the middle of the forest where there was a hut belonging to a very powerful soothsayer. He was able to predict the future with accuracy.

The young prince introduced himself and asked the soothsayer to tell them how they can find their way back to the village. He did and asked if they would like to know what was awaiting them in the future.

The young prince obliged, and the soothsayer told him he was going to be a great king. His reign would be marked with abundance and peace.

He asked his friend if he also would want to know what was awaiting him in the future and the young friend declined saying he was not interested. His friend the prince persuaded him to let the soothsayer tell him about his future. After much persuasion he obliged.

The soothsayer told him he was going to be very poor. In fact, he was going to be the poorest in the village.

As they left for the village the prince consoled him. Well, you have me as your friend, no matter how bad the future would be for you I will be there. I will make things better for you. To his surprise his friend the pauper kept saying 'I will not be poor'.

'I will not be poor', became his nickname. He started planting farmlands. At a point his friend the prince told him he was overworking himself. You will work yourself to death he said, all the friend could say was 'I will not be poor'.

Years past and the prince was now king, but his friend did not become the poorest in the village. Instead, he became the richest man in the village having so many cultivated farmlands.

Then came a serious famine in the village and several neighboring villages. The only man having crops for sale was the farmer who once was a pauper now the richest man.

People gave all they had (money, houses, bicycles, even children as servants) to him to get food.

At a point the villagers asked he become their king which he declined. His friend the king did not understand how he was able to twist his fortune, so he went into the forest to seek the soothsayer who had foretold the future for them.

When the King asked the soothsayer what had happened, all the soothsayer said was 'your friend had taken the antidote to poverty'.

Hard work is the only medicine to poverty.

In my journey in life, I have come to know that there are two things God cannot do. One is that he cannot lie, secondly, he cannot help a lazy man.

All you need my friend is hard work. Remember, your dream is only a dream until you give life to it. No matter how beautiful your dream is, if you don't work it out it will remain but a dream. Give life to your dream today, work for it.

Start now, no matter how small. Get started, no matter how little. In the book of Zechariah chapter 4:10, the Bible warns against despising the days of small beginnings.

Here is clear evidence that hard work pays off and slothfulness does not. The diligent one who works hard will be the one who can be trusted to be in charge but the slothful one will be forced to labor for others, perhaps for the diligent one. Hard work pays off in the end. Most employers take notice of the one who works hard but also the one who doesn't work hard (is slothful or lazy) usually doesn't slip past the attention of the one who rules either (or is the boss).

Jesus was a carpenter and carpenters in those days didn't just mean woodwork but working with large timbers and stones and all of it was manual labor and of course without the aid of any power tools so everything was done by hand. Jesus said "My Father is always working, and so am I" (John 5:17) and so must we be. We must all work so that we won't be in hunger, and we can work to help those who cannot work for themselves for various reasons. The Bible has much to say about laziness and idleness …and none of it is good.

The Bible said in the book of Proverbs 13:4 (AMP),'
The soul (appetite) of the lazy person craves and gets nothing [for lethargy overcomes ambition],
But the soul (appetite) of the diligent [who works willingly] is rich *and* abundantly supplied.

It is good to dream and dreaming big. But your dream is only a dream until you give life to it. For your dream to come alive you must take action, 'work for it'.

Mary Kay said,' we must succeed if we don't then we must work for somebody for the rest of our lives'.

In life you must be focused, you must stand for something, or you will fall for anything. You must have a mental strength. Samson was strong physically but lacked the mental strength. A man without a mental strength cannot be disciplined. It was the lack of focus that gave Gehazi in the Bible his dwelling place in the congregation of the lepers.

Nothing in the world is worse than someone who doesn't understand what he possesses, not long he would forget who he is.

Many of us are fond of giving excuses for our inadequacies- My parents were bad, my education was interrupted and my uncle who was supposed to be my only hope failed, they just don't love me.

Beloved you don't have any excuse to live below your purpose.

God is looking for men who are focused. Men who would shun distractions and lounge into the deep.

If you want to get a net breaking catch this year, just like Peter get to the other side and get hold of the ultimate- your focus.

Lazy people have a habit for getting done all the things that are not true priorities. But when it comes to the hard stuff, they suddenly find every reason why they could not complete the task.

That's because hard stuff is, well, "hard." It is a priority for a reason, and that's because it is the thing that's going to move the needle. But often times, what moves the needle lies in the unknown. It requires a risk, or a leap of faith, in some way.

Those who are successful at what they do know this. And instead of shying away from the challenge, they make themselves do these "hard tasks" first--before allowing themselves the luxury of the easy stuff.

Proverbs 6:9-11(AMP),' How long will you lie down, O lazy one? When will you arise from your sleep [and learn self-discipline]?[10] "Yet a little sleep, a little slumber,
A little folding of the hands to lie down *and* rest"—[11] So your poverty will come like an *approaching* prowler who walks [slowly, but surely] And your need [will come] like an armed man [making you helpless].

2 Thessalonians 3:6 (NIV): "In the name of the Lord Jesus Christ, we command you, brothers and sisters, to keep away from every believer who is idle and disruptive and does not live according to the teaching you received from us."

Paul commands believers to avoid anyone "who is walking in idleness and not in accordance with the tradition that they received from him." In other words, those who walk in idleness were apparently siphoning off of others who do work. This was not "in accord with the tradition that [they] received from" Paul. Paul later wrote "If anyone is not willing to work, let him not eat" (2 Thessalonians 3:10). These are the people we should avoid. There are so many "get rich" schemes out there that so many get entangled in because they simply don't want to work hard like most people do.

Any money you didn't work for, you don't have the wisdom to manage it. That's why many lottery winners after their wins just some couple of months after, they are back to square one-they are broke again.

Paul commanded believers to "do their work quietly and to earn their own living" and not support the idle ones (2 Thessalonians 3:12b).

There is a difference between working hard and laboring. When a man is laboring it means he is working hard but has nothing to show for it. It means working hard as an elephant but eating like an ant. God does not wish this for us and that is why Jesus gave a call in the book of Matthew 11:28(KJV), - Come unto me, all ye that labour and are heavy laden, and I will give you rest.

On the other hand, when a man is working hard it means he has something to show for his labor. When you hear someone say, 'I have been working since morning and forgot to take my break', and he is happy about it, then he was indeed working hard. Work hard for your dream my friend, the joy you have when you see your dream come through cannot be explained in words, it is overwhelming.

Be Diligent at work, so many are willing and ready to Pray and fast for their status to change but a lot are not ready to improve themselves at what they do. Proverbs 22:29(KJV), - Seest thou a man diligent in his business? He shall stand before kings; he shall not stand before mean men.

Proverbs 6:6(KJV), "Go to the ant, thou sluggard; consider her ways, and be wise. Proverbs 30:25 "The ants are a people not strong, yet they prepare their meat in the summer.

It is impossible to direct a ship which is not in motion, but if it's in motion a little tilt from the rudder you will be able to point that ship to any direction of your choice. God will not be able to assist you if you are doing nothing, He won't be able to direct you if you are not moving.

The little in your hand becomes a lot in the hand of God. He asked Moses,' what's in your hand', and Moses answered,' a rod'. That ordinary rod in the hand of Moses became a powerful tool in the hand of God. The same rod was used to path the sea. What is in your hand? What are you doing with your hand?

In my years of pastoring youths and young adults, there were instances I would ask a young man, what are you doing and the answer I get is 'nothing'. I just wondered what someone can be doing, and that thing is called 'Nothing'.

I always told them, 'Stop doing nothing, start doing something'.

Money is not just a means of exchange but a measure of value. It is not a scarce resource, but the idea to earn money is, and it comes to those who produce value. It is only the man that creates value that is said to be valuable. When your value increases Money will definitely increase. When you are able to provide the solutions to people's problem, they become your ATM machines.

Stop complaining of all that is not working and start providing the solutions to the numerous problems and challenges confronting us. America was built by men who saw a challenge and decided to provide the solutions. You are not paid because you showed up in the office, but you should be paid because we had a challenge, we hired you and you fixed it.

Recession is not a time when money is scarce but a time when money locates its rightful owners, men who provide value. What is your value?

In chapter one I described the attitudes of the Jacobs and the Esau's. And I did say the Esau's are lazy people because they can't roast that which they caught. They have dreams but can't bring it to pass because they don't work for it. They don't like getting their hands dirty. They sell the future for what they need now. The Jacobs on the other hands will do everything to keep their dreams alive. They buy the future by working for it.

The Esau's don't want any challenge (Esau caught a game but couldn't cook it-laziness); always have excuses, why they need to remain where they are. He does not want to discover anything new, do anything new. Not ready to take up new challenges, sees life as a big risk.

The Esau generation - A generation that will sell their future for what they will eat today. A generation that will go after a game when they catch it, they devour it. They turn a forest into a desert. God says He hates Esau and loves Jacob.

The Jacobs ask God for a tree and turn it to a forest. They spot opportunities in the midst of oppositions. They buy the future by delayed gratification. According to Warren Buffett, "someone is sitting under the shade of a tree today because someone sometimes past planted a tree". The question for you today is, "are you planting the trees?" Your children coming behind will they have a tree to sit under its shade?

In life, we need to learn how to stretch never wanting to settle for anything that is not more, exceeding and above all we ever ask or think. Ephesians 3:20. -Now unto him that is able to do exceeding abundantly above all that we ask or think, according to the power that worketh in us,

Tommy Lasorda said, "The difference between the Impossible and possible lies in the Persons determination".

Colonel Sanders, the founder of KFC started his dream at 65 years old. After retirement from the force, he got a social security cheque for only $105 and was mad. Instead of complaining he did something about it.

He thought restaurant owners would love his fried chicken recipe, use it, sales would increase, and he'd get a percentage of it. He drove around the country knocking on doors, sleeping in his car, wearing his white suit.

Do you know how many times people said NO, till he got one yes? 1009 times!

Decide what is important to you and take huge steps everyday even though it doesn't seem like it's working. Success doesn't happen without failures. It's reality.

DEAL WITH IT

No list of success from failures would be complete without mentioning the name Thomas Edison, the man who gave us many inventions including the light bulb. He knew failure wouldn't stop him. According to him, he said,' if I find 10,000 ways something won't work, I haven't failed. I am not discouraged, because every wrong attempt discarded is another step forward.

Everything that you need to succeed in life is already in you. You are not inferior to anybody. Only the best is good enough for you. Don't ever settle for good enough. If better is possible, good is not enough. There is a level higher than where you are now.

Don't go for a C when God can give you an A. You have been tied down for too long it is time to lose yourself.

How bad do you want to achieve your dream? Is it better to be so bad that rejection won't derail you?

If you don't give up, keep dreaming, keep pushing, little by little, God will bring it to pass. For the fact that it didn't happen last year does not mean it can't still happen this year. Your best is yet to come.

I heard the story of this man who bought a plot of land and built a small structure in front with hope that sometime in the future when he had gathered some amount of money, he would build a bigger structure behind for his family.

Eventually, he was able to raise the money but when it was time to build, they discovered that there was a big boulder (a large mass of stone) in the ground. They could not bring in a heavy machinery because of the building he had erected in front. So, every morning and evening he would take a hammer and go to the boulder and pray. While praying he would be hitting the boulder, asking it to scatter.

His wife and children always make fun of him whenever they see him walk to the boulder to pray. But one day something remarkable happened. The man screamed, his family taught something evil had happened to him, so they rushed to where he was, lo and behold the boulder was shattered in pieces.

What he didn't know was that each day he hit the boulder with the hammer, even though nothing seems to be happening on the outside, internally it was breaking apart. And eventually it scattered as a result of the culmination of the several hits the man was giving to it morning and night.

Once again, your destiny is indeed in your hand. It is time you begin to work it out. It's your responsibility to get up. Life is 10% what you are dealt with and 90% how you respond to what you were dealt with.

Your challenge doesn't equal your promises from God- Your best is yet to come.

We will conclude this chapter with two quotes, one from Ralph Marston, which says,' don't lower your expectations to meet your performance, instead raise your level of performance to meet your expectation. Expect the best of yourself, and then do what is necessary to make it a reality.

"Perseverance is the hard work you do after you get tired of doing the hard work you already did" …Newt Gingrich.

CHAPTER EIGHT

EXPECT IT

There is a very thin line between Success and failure. And there is also a very slight difference between successful people and unsuccessful people: **Successful people make decision quickly and change them rarely; Unsuccessful people make decisions slowly and change them quickly.**

People do say life is not fair and I say yes. And in not being fair to us all, it becomes fair.

We all have one head, two eyes, two ears, two hands and two legs. What you do with what God gave you is left up to you. The person sitting beside you has no more than you do, he could have done more with what he had. But he didn't get any more.

There is an adage which says, 'to whom much is given, much is expected'. In life your expectation determines what you get. If your expectation is small your getting will be small. If your expectation is great, your getting becomes great.

You cannot have what you cannot see, hence the need to have a big dream.

"If you expect nothing from somebody you are never disappointed." ... "Blessed is he who expects nothing, for he shall never be disappointed." Pope Alexander

Treat a man as he is, and he will remain as he is. Treat a man as he can and should be and he will become as he can and should be." Steven Covey

I would like to complete this book with the story of the woman with the issue of blood in the book of Mark chapter 5:25-34, the story is a sad story which had a happy ending. Her story encourages us that no matter how bad our story may be, it can also have a happy ending.

We can identify with her circumstance in these present times. For example, all the things you see are just expenses and nothing new or no business is coming your way. You are making a lot of efforts, but nothing to show for it; lots of activities, but no reward, no promotion, no progress made, etc. Or you may have spent money, sent out proposals, waited month after month, year after year for the fruit of the womb, searched for jobs with no headway, but there are no results, and people are beginning to ask you "Where is your God?" God is telling you that your story will change. Your testimony will silence all your enemies and mockers very soon in Jesus Mighty name.

(Micah 7:8-10), (NIV)- Do not gloat over me, my enemy!
  Though I have fallen, I will rise.
Though I sit in darkness,
  the LORD will be my light.
9 Because I have sinned against him,
  I will bear the LORD's wrath,
until he pleads my case
  and upholds my cause.
He will bring me out into the light;

I will see his righteousness.
¹⁰ Then my enemy will see it
  and will be covered with shame,
she who said to me,
  "Where is the LORD your God?"
My eyes will see her downfall;
  even now she will be trampled underfoot
  like mire in the streets.

The woman with the issue of blood was hemorrhaging for 12 years, she was unclean and anything she touched became unclean (Leviticus 15:25-27), she was cut off from society and every religious meeting, it means that even the church could not help her. She was rich but her situation sapped her of all her money and energy. She spent everything that she had, but her situation grew worse. She visited many doctors but there was no cure. She became broke and had low self-esteem.

In the midst of it all, God gave her ears that could hear. He sent to her destiny helpers - (these are people who will usually wake you up to your destiny in life), people who do not gossip and spread bad news, but who genuinely had her interest at heart and sought solution for her plight. Mark 5:27, says she heard that only Jesus could heal, save, deliver, calm every storm, fight all the battles of life, open doors that have been shut and shut doors that need to be shut in one's life, lift up, promote, reward with the fruit of womb, divinely connect, etc. She then made up her mind to seek after Jesus Christ the Healer. The same Jesus is alive today and ready to help you only if you can also believe in Him and call upon Him.

She also heard what Jesus said in Matthew 11:28; **"Come unto Me, all ye that labour and are heavy**

laden, and I will give you rest." Due to her condition, someone must have told her that God is close to the broken-hearted and the crushed in spirit (Psalm 34:18). She would have then decided to meet Jesus and tell Him about all her problems. As you tell Jesus about your problems, challenges today, you will not be disappointed; He will lift your burdens today and you will testify.

HER FAITH INCREASED

The Bible says as the woman heard all the testimonies of what God had done, her faith welled up. Romans 10:17 says; "So then faith cometh by hearing, and hearing by the word of God." As you have heard what God has done in Scriptures and what He is doing in our contemporary times, your faith should increase. You should be encouraged because God is no respecter of persons. This same God Who has been healing, promoting and saving is your God and will meet you at the point of your need in Jesus Mighty name.

This woman had faith that if she went to meet Jesus, He would heal her. Remember that FAITH is you saying and acting on that which you believe. She had a mental picture of her healing. Faith sees the answer, and the solution. As you begin to visualize and expect your breakthroughs, miracles this month, the Bible says in Proverbs 23:18 **"for surely there is an end; and thine expectation shall not be cut off."** She had expectation. My question for you today is, do you have any expectation?

WHAT IS EXPECTATION?

It is aiming one's attention at an object with concentration, with intensity and with eagerness. Expectation can be referred to as a hope, confidence, looking forward to a glorious future, a strong belief that something good is about to happen or things will surely change and get better.

Expectation also means looking forward to something that is about to happen. For example, when a woman is pregnant, people say she is expectant, meaning she is looking forward to when her baby will be born. When you have expectations, it ignites a sense of anticipation that will motivate you to action, just as expectation motivated the woman in the reference text, causing her to get up, against all odds (defying her weakness, her social stigma, etc.), to come out to look for Jesus.

Expectation also means turning the eyes away from everything else and focusing on an object alone. This is what happened to the father of the prodigal son in Luke 15:20. The son had been gone for many years, but the father must have been standing on a tower looking out for him. He had an expectation, he had prayed and believed God. He was always on the lookout- looking for something good to happen. When the son was afar off on his way back home, the father saw him because he had been watching out for him. This tells us that *you don't wait to see a change, you watch to see a change* because the Bible in Matthew 26:41 says, **"Watch and pray."**

Anticipation, being a state of heightened expectation gets you up and makes you watch because your change is surely coming. Psalm 123:1-2 says **"Unto thee lift I up mine eyes, O thou that dwells in the heavens. Behold, as the eyes of servants look unto the hand of their masters, and as the eyes of a maiden unto the hand of her mistress; so, our eyes wait upon the LORD our God, until that He have mercy upon us."**

This implies that you should concentrate, be on the lookout, be expectant, lift up your eyes, and be focused on God, your Helper who will meet you at the point of your need. As you do so, God will answer you in Jesus Mighty name.

You need to have a mental picture of your expectation. *Is your anticipation strong enough to move you to take an action?* Do you see your situation turning around for the better? You need to have that mental picture of what you expect because that is what the woman with the issue of blood had. Your expectations today should depend upon the Word and the promise of God. Psalm 62:5 says, **"My soul, wait thou only upon God; for my expectation is from Him."**

God can never fail, and He can never lie, hence, you will not be disappointed. If God says something, expect that it would come to pass because He is not man to lie or the son of man to repent.

Numbers 23:19, (KJV)- God is not a man, that he should lie; neither the son of man, that he should repent: hath he said, and shall he not do it? Or hath he spoken, and shall he not make it good?

Jeremiah 32:27 says **"Behold, I am the LORD, the God of all flesh: is there anything too hard for me?"** Jesus in Mark 9:23 said **"If you can believe, all things are possible to him that believes."** All things are possible to the believer. That is why Psalm 33:9 says, **"For He spoke, and it was done; He commanded, and it stood fast."**

What is your expectation?

In Mark 5:28 [AMP], we see that the anticipation of this woman motivated her to keep saying to herself that, **"If I only touch His garments, I shall be restored to health."** She had seen the mental picture, she had heard, she expected, she anticipated it and it motivated her to break through the crowd and touch the hem of Jesus' garment. As she touched the hem of His garment, she touched the heart of Jesus.

As you seek Jesus today, you will touch His heart and He will turn around to answer you. Proverbs 23:18 says **"For surely there is an end; and thine expectation shall not be cut off."** There is an end to your sorrow, to every challenge that you might be facing, every pain, joblessness, weeping, barrenness, stagnancy in Jesus Name. You need an expectation today, you need to imagine it today, and you need a picture of your glorious tomorrow today because God will perform His good Word towards you.

DREAM BIG because we serve a BIG God. As you begin to have great expectations, see it and act towards it, and God will go ahead of you to prepare everything that you require for your dream to come true. It is God who will do it, stop thinking, don't bother yourself about how He will do it. It will be unto you according to your great expectation in Jesus Mighty name.

WHAT SHOULD YOUR EXPECTATIONS BE?

1. You should expect to be healed because the Bible says in Isaiah 55:3 that **"By His stripes we are healed."** This is based on the promise of God. Jeremiah 17:14- Heal me, LORD, and I will be healed; save me and I will be saved, for you are the one I praise.

2. You should expect to meet your life partner because Isaiah 34:16 says **"...None shall want her mate."**, and Genesis 2:18 says that **"It is not good that the man should be alone; I will make him a help meet for him."**

3. You should expect to be fruitful and have your own children because Psalm 127:3 says **"...the fruit of the womb is His reward."**

4. You should expect to prosper because Philippians 4:19 says **"And my God will supply all your needs according to His riches in glory in Christ Jesus."**

5. You should expect to be promoted because Psalm 75:6 says, **"Promotion comes from God."**

6. You should expect total security and no accidents because Isaiah 57:14 says, **"No weapon that is fashioned against you shall prosper."**

7. You should expect victory even without a fight because Deuteronomy 28:7 says, **"The Lord shall cause thine enemies that rise up against thee to be smitten before thy face: they shall come out against thee one way and flee before thee seven ways."**

So, stop running away from your challenges. You cannot overcome what you cannot confront. For the fact that you are small inside does not mean you don't have a great call. When you start running for one thing you will start running for everything. Stop running and face what you need to face and deal with what you need to deal with.

During the 1992 Barcelona Summer Olympics, a young American Derek Redmond was favored to win the 400 meters race. However, disappointment came about 250 meters from the finish. His hamstring tore, he went to the ground in pains. As the medics brought the stretcher to pick him, he got up, despite the pain he decided to finish the race hopping.

Suddenly his father Jim, pushed through the security, came to him, and told him, "You don't have to do this", and his weeping son replied, "Yes I do". Well then, replied to his father "we are going to do this together".

The father wrapped his arms around his son and helped him hobble through the track. Shortly before the finish line, the father let go of his son, and the son completed the race with a standing ovation from the crowd of 65,000.

Derek Redmond may not have won any medal that day, but he managed to finish his race. Today his story stands out as the real face of the Olympics. Despite the pain, despite the tears, he determined to give his all.

When his father saw his struggle, his pain, he went down to help his son.

God sees your pain, when we are hurt and fighting to finish, He comes and helps us.

Life is indeed a race, and the race of life is not for the strong. Without God there will be some things you will not be able to accomplish on your own.

In the book of Genesis 27:20 (KJV), -And Isaac said unto his son, how is it that thou hast found it so quickly, my son? And he said, because the LORD thy God brought it to me. Except God bring some things to you, you will only struggle in vain.

Psalms 127:1-2(KJV), - Except the LORD build the house, they labour in vain that build it: except the LORD keep the city, the watchman waketh but in vain.

[2] It is vain for you to rise up early, to sit up late, to eat the bread of sorrows: for so he giveth his beloved sleep.

He loves you and wants to help you. He sees your struggle, he sees your pain, He sees your tears. Call on Him today.

Jeremiah 29:11 (NIV)-For I know the plans I have for you," declares the LORD, "plans to prosper you and not to harm you, plans to give you hope and a future.

Life will always want to push you down but if you can hold on to God, you will always fight your way back up. It is never over until you win. The call of God is a call to excellence not a call to mediocrity. If anything is worth doing, it is worth doing well. If you can't do it with excellence, don't bother doing it at all.

There must be persistency for God's direction. The Bible says in Proverbs 19:21(KJV)-There are many devices in a man's heart; nevertheless, the counsel of the LORD that shall stand.

Psalms 32: 8-(KJV) -I will instruct thee and teach thee in the way which thou shalt go: I will guide thee with my eye.

It is only when we know what God wants us to do that, we will have total confidence that what we are attempting is right and God is on our side.

Direction is a matter of fact; ideas are a matter of opinion. Direction from God is not possible without Him. Look beyond what you see with your natural eyes. Listen with your spiritual ears. Keep your antenna up for God's perfect direction in your life.

Divine direction is really heard not seen. We should be more interested in the unseen than in the seen. God is much interested in your success. As we conclude this tour together, I live you with these two scriptures:

James 4:2 (KJV)-Ye lust, and have not: ye kill, and desire to have, and cannot obtain: ye fight and war, yet ye have not, because ye ask not.

Proverbs 3:5(KJV)-Trust in the LORD with all thine heart; and lean not unto thine own understanding.

Once again, I will encourage you to call on Him in prayers, amazing things start happening when we start praying. Prayer time is never wasted, Jeremiah 33:3, - Call unto me, and I will answer thee, and show thee great and mighty things, which thou knowest not.

Do you trust God enough to know that your set time are in your future? A set time for you to be completely well. A set time for that breakthrough a set time to meet the right person. The appointed time are already set in your calendar. You can trust God's timing. If it has not happened yet, it does not mean that something is wrong, or God is mad at you. It does not mean it is not going to work out. God has established the time to the split second. Your step is ordered by the creator of the Universe.

Keep believing, don't give up, and keep holding on and very soon it will be your turn to laugh. Your past may be on the tongues of others, but your future is in the hand of God.

In life you might get knocked down, but always remember that the winners jump back to the fight, only the losers stay down.

In Isaiah 40:31(NIV)- but those who hope in the LORD
   will renew their strength.
They will soar on wings like eagles;
   they will run and not grow weary,
   they will walk and not be faint.

There are challenges in life that overwhelm the strongest of people, fears that gnaw at the stoutest of human hearts, and youths who grow faint and weary. They stumble and fall because they rely on their own inner strength and human resources, which are not really a sufficient shield in the storms of life. Only power from above is sufficient to sustain us. Only God's protective hand can shelter us from the storms of life and not our own limited, human abilities.

God spoke In Isaiah 46:4 (NIV)- Even to your old age and grey hairs
  I am he; I am he who will sustain you.
I have made you and I will carry you;
  I will sustain you and I will rescue you.

Here we see that God has made a promise to carry us all through even to our old age. All we need to do is dependent on Him for He is reliable, dependable, and faithful.

God's greatness is not just that he is strong, but that he is strong for us.

Peradventure you have never had any encounter with Jesus before, I will want to give you an opportunity to do so.

God's glory will not come into your life because of sin but the glory can be restored if Christ is in you because Colossians 1:27 says **"To whom God would make known what the riches of the glory of this mystery is among the Gentiles, which is Christ in you, the hope of glory."**

If you are willing to repent and surrender your life to Jesus Christ, then say this prayer right now:

LORD Jesus, I come to You right now, I know I am a sinner, please forgive me my sins. With my mouth, I confess that Jesus, from right now, you are the **LORD** of my life. Change my heart from a heart that is disobedient to a heart that obeys You. With my new heart, I believe that it is because of me that You came to this world; You died for my sins, You took away my sins. Take away my problems also, write my name in the Book of Life, make me brand new, and meet me at the point of my expectation in Jesus Mighty Name.